AN ASTROLOGICAL GUIDE TO SELF-AWARENESS

Donna Cunningham

CRCS PUBLICATIONS
Post Office Box 20850
RENO, NEVADA 89515
U.S.A.

Library of Congress Cataloging in Publication Data

Cunningham, Donna, 1942-
    An astrological guide to self-awareness.

    1. Astrology and psychology.   I. Title.
BF1729.P8C86   133.5   78-57820
ISBN 0-916360-09-1

© 1978 by Donna Cunningham

FIRST EDITION

INTERNATIONAL STANDARD BOOK NUMBER: 0-916360-09-1

LIBRARY OF CONGRESS CATALOG CARD NUMBER: 78-57820

Published simultaneously in the United States
and Canada by CRCS Publications

*Distributed in the United States &
Internationally by CRCS Publications*

Cover Design by Armando Busick

Book Design by Joan M. Case and Kathleen Mullins

Editorial Consultant: Barbara McEnerney

Contents

This book is fondly dedicated
to the two people who
have most influenced my
thinking on astrology:

ROD CHASE
and
RICHARD IDEMAN

---

* The word "their" is often used in this book where "his" would traditionally be used because of the neutral quality of "their" in contrast to "his" as an exclusively masculine pronoun. In some cases, however, "his" is still used, even though it may refer to a person of either sex, when the use of "their" seemed much too awkward.

PART ONE
ASTROLOGY &
SELF-AWARENESS

INTRODUCTION
THE STARS ARE NOT TO BLAME

So that you'll know where I'm coming from as you read this book, I would like to say some things about my approach to astrology. That way you can take my particular biases into account in deciding whether or not you agree with me. My bias is toward psychological understanding of the behavior and traits described by the chart. I do not, in short, believe in using the birth chart as the best of all possible cop-outs. ("I can't help drinking, Judge, I'm a Pisces.") It is a great tool for understanding people—for finding their strengths as well as their weaknesses and hang-ups—and I do feel therapists would get results much faster if they zeroed in on the chart. I also believe that we *can* get better, that we can stop behaving in neurotic and self-destructive ways and that the chart can help by pointing up more constructive uses of our basic traits.

My second bias, implicit in the one above, is that the stars are not to blame.[1] I believe that our lives are not controlled by things out there, but are shaped by our own thought patterns. The planets only reflect what is going on, like a mirror. Just as the mirror does not cause you to go gray, the planets do not cause bad things to happen to you. *You* make bad things happen to you by your self-defeating, neurotic, rebellious, or neglectful behavior. If you get fired, it's easy to blame that goldarned Uranus crossing your Midheaven. But why not blame yourself for all those times you came in late? STOP PASSING THE BUCK! Likewise, the planets do not cause *good* things to happen either. We bring them about by our attitudes of openness and faith in life.

---

1. This section reprinted from my editorial in the September '77 issue of *Astrology Today*. © 1977 CBS Publications, the Consumer Publishing Division of CBS, Inc.

You may be saying, "If this is true, then what is the point of astrology?" That's like asking a surgeon what's the point of a diagnostic x-ray. Or an architect what all those blueprints are for. Or an ordinary tourist why he needs a road map. The chart *is* a sort of map to show you the way. . . it's not the chart's fault if you make a wrong turn or elect not to take the best route. In other occult studies, we seem to recognize more readily that the tool doesn't create the problem but only maps out the terrain and points the way. In palmistry, for instance, we realize that a line on the palm does not *cause* you to live your life in a certain way, it only reflects the fact that you *do* live that way. Nor do we feel that the act of dealing a Tarot card spread *causes* a situation to come out the way the cards say; we see that the cards only reflect and describe what the situation can be if you follow a certain course of action. If you choose to alter your behavior, the situation can change.

The *I Ching* clearly operates on this principle. You throw three coins six times and come up with a pattern called a hexagram, whose meaning you look up in a book. If the hexagram is unfavorable and you choose to persevere in the unwise course of action, you are not going to blame the consequences on those three little coins you tossed, are you? To go to an even greater extreme, let's consider tea leaves. Predictions can be made from them, but surely the tea leaves are not to blame if you don't heed their warnings. People don't go around saying things like, "My life was just wonderful until I drank that cup of tea"—unless, of course, there was arsenic in it! So why do we accept it when people go around saying things like, "Neptune has totally ruined my life," or "Saturn has destroyed my marriage."

A case in point is horary astrology. For those of you who aren't familiar with this branch of astrology, it involves asking a question ("Will I get the job?" "What happened to the missing money?" "Will my boyfriend return to me?") and then setting up a chart for the time the question entered your mind. The answer to the question and a great deal of information about the situation is contained in the chart. I don't think that any astrologer would say that setting up the horary chart *caused* things to turn out the way they did. But why should horary charts work any differently than any other chart? Either the planets in the horary chart caused the misfortune to happen (in which case they should pass a law against practicing horary astrology), or else the planets in *natal* charts don't cause our problems either—you can't have it both ways. It's far better to say that all charts are *descriptive*. The chart does describe you, but it does not *cause* you to be that way, nor does it limit you to a negative expression of your potential, if that is where you are now.

Another bias I have is preferring not to rely on karma to explain away the things that happen to us. While I definitely believe in reincarnation, in practice I find it useless to speculate about. We just don't have the wisdom to know why certain experiences or certain people are sent into our lives. . . or, if we can dimly discern the reason, it is often only from the perspective of time and distance. I feel that many times "punishment" isn't the point at all—certain painful experiences are sent to help us grow into stronger people and to push us out of the ruts we've gotten into. A lot of the pain, too, is of our own doing in *this* life—nobody told you to keep on beating your head against the wall. Such experiences are not karma but neurosis—self-defeating patterns of behavior that we keep on repeating long after we should have learned better. "Karma" is often just a label that we use to avoid examining our own part in creating a painful experience. . . another wonderful cop-out.

Unfortunately, many people do use astrology to cop-out, just like people who study a little psychology and spend the rest of their lives blaming their parents for what's wrong with them. The astro cop-outs, though, are shifting the blame on a grander level—"the stars." And what a superlative excuse it is—who'd expect you to straighten out your life when you can say the mess is due to something as big and as far out of your control as Neptune or Uranus? The evolved (or more accurately, evolving) person will learn the same thing from both astrology and psychology—that as adults we have the ultimate responsibility for ourselves. The external events and conditions in our lives are what we attract to ourselves through our inner conflicts, needs, and attitudes, be they conscious or unconscious. Wrong thinking and wrong actions are at the root of most of our troubles. Start examining your own thoughts, actions, and emotions in a problem situation to see how you contribute to or provoke the mistreatment you get.

To believe that you are being buffeted by Pluto or held back by some bad aspect is very short-sighted. What you should see from the various chapters in this book is that every difficult thing in the chart can lead us to positive, constructive insights and actions that will help us move along on the spiritual path. We generally grow through the mastery of the adverse circumstances, inner conflicts and difficult times that we go through. With that in mind, you can regard difficult aspects, transits, and sign placements as opportunities to grow. The true usefulness of a chart, as I see it, is to get a better perspective on yourself, to appreciate your own individuality and potential, and to work toward your most positive expression of self. Your chart is only an instrument panel where you take readings on the course of your life. YOU ARE STILL THE PILOT!

CHAPTER 1

ASTROLOGY
A TOOL FOR SELF-AWARENESS

Astrology has two helpful functions. One is to identify the strengths and abilities we have which we can capitalize on. For instance, it was only by studying astrology and getting repeated encouragement from astrologers that I came to have faith in myself as a potential writer. Before that, I considered myself a lousy poet and left it at that. I'm still a lousy poet, but astrology gave me the courage to try other kinds of writing that have been more successful and fulfilling. My knowledge of astrology, then, resulted in a change in the direction of my career and life.

The second function, and the one we will focus on in this chapter, is to help us identify the ways we create our own problems and cause unhappiness for ourselves and those around us. As we saw in the introduction, my belief is that planets are not responsible for our happiness or unhappiness, they only point out the ways we have been causing our self-fulfillment or self-defeat. And, if self-defeating behaviors are causing problems for us, we can use the chart as a guide to facing them honestly and directly. If we do so, we can tackle those problem areas and ultimately realize the most positive potential of every placement and every aspect in our charts. Self-defeat is far more of a problem for most of us than anything an outsider can inflict. Do you know the ways you are your own worst enemy? Traditionally, astrologers have looked at the twelfth house for the answer to this question, but I feel the whole chart should be surveyed. All those difficult sign and house placements and all those troublesome aspects will show you how you're contributing to your own problems.

The self-defeating patterns in our lives are like patterns you use in making dresses. The same one can be used over and over again. The dresses may look a little different because of variations in material, color, or length, but it's basically the same pattern. Likewise, the people you get involved with romantically (or, likewise, as friends, or in work situations) might look a bit different in the beginning but wind up being alike in the end. For instance, one woman who wrote to my advice column had been married three times and all three of her husbands beat her. I told her that three abusive husbands were an embarrassment of riches, that she was choosing these men, and that unless she got into therapy, I could confidently predict that the next man she got hooked up with would beat her too. My prediction wasn't based on astrology, it just stood to reason.

Once you can identify a pattern of self-defeating behavior, however, the chart can lead you to an understanding of exactly what is behind it and how to begin correcting it. A problem in love? Look at Venus, the seventh house, and its ruler. Communication blocks keep you from being understood? Look at Mercury, the third house, and its ruler. Trace it all the way back to its roots—it's not enough to say that Mercury in Scorpio shows that you are reserved about expressing your feelings outwardly. How did you get that way? The chart can tell you that, too, if you look at it psychologically. This book has many examples of psychological analysis.

One of the more common roots of self-defeat and probably the most devastating is self-hatred. Self-hatred is one of the most painful emotions you can feel. It is also one of the most crippling, because when you hate yourself, you act in ways that lead others to reject you or in self-defeating ways that cause you to fail. The rejections and failures then make you hate yourself even more. How can you break out of this cycle? By trying to find out what causes the self-hatred and then getting past it to accept and finally to love yourself. I doubt if any psychotherapist would quarrel with that, and psychotherapy *may* be needed to accomplish this deceptively simple-sounding thing.[1] I do think, however, that astrology and a thorough understanding of your chart can help in this process. The person's natal horoscope can

1. This section reprinted by permission of Sterling Publications. It appeared in the 1/78 issue of *Astrology Guide* under my pen name, Marisol Malone, as "Your Way to a Happier Personality—Self Acceptance & Astrology."©1978 by Sterling Publications.

give a short-cut by identifying those nebulous, generally unconscious, and often irrational-seeming conflicts within the person which lead to self-hatred.

Sometimes we only get at our self-hatred by indirect means—examining what we hate in others. We have all probably had the experience of taking an immediate and powerful dislike to someone we just met. . . and maybe had it pointed out to us none too kindly that we disliked that person precisely because they were too much like us in some unpleasant way. What we reacted to so strongly in them was actually something in ourselves that we don't like to face up to.

This goes for sun signs as well. Richard Ideman, a profound astrological thinker, has pointed out that the signs you hate tell a great deal—not necessarily about the sign per se—but *about yourself.* By the psychological mechanism of *projection,* we "disown" parts of ourselves that we don't approve of or are uncomfortable with and assign them to someone or some group outside ourselves. "Me? Yearning to be passive and helpless instead of so darned self-sufficient? No, it's *those Pisces!*" (Stereotypes and prejudices are based on projections such as these, and perhaps astrological prejudices could become the prejudices of the New Age, now that we're "too enlightened" for the old ethnic ones.)

You may be amused by an illustration of astrological projection, the mechanism which Richard Ideman has identified so well, at work in one of the astrology classes I taught, a group of ardent feminists. A couple of the students began talking about the signs they hated. On instinct, I asked one of them, "What sign do you dislike most?"

"Oh, Geminis! They're disgusting!"

"What sign is your father?" I hazarded.

"Gemini!"

I went around the room like that, asking each of them what sign she disliked most. Dramatically, each one of them, myself included, named the sun sign of her father. Now this would only be an amusing curiosity, possibly revealing something about the roots of our feminism, if it were not for one tragic fact. Our parents, as shapers of ourselves, are part of our charts and part of our character. I may not be a Pisces, as my father was, but my Sun is in a water sign and located in the twelfth house, making me not unlike him. The fact that I generally do not like Pisces says that I dislike a very important part of myself, and that I need to get in touch with that part and reconcile it with the rest of me in order to be truly healthy.

You, too, are probably carrying around in your chart the signs you love to hate. Look for them in unsuspected places. If you have Sun conjunct Jupiter but can't bear Sagittarians, look out—you are practically a Sag yourself. If you hate Aries with a passion but have Mars on the Ascendant, then you hate the aggressive, competitive part of yourself. Can't stand Gemini? Isn't that where you have your South Node? Virgos set your teeth on edge? Strange, with a stellium in the sixth house, you have such a lot in common! Look for the signs you hate in your own chart— you may find out you are projecting an important part of yourself.

Then there is what I call the Sunday School or confessional brand of self-hatred. . . so named because it happens periodically, when we feel called upon to examine our faults, and because it generally has a moralistic cast to it. "Why am I so *BAD*? What makes me do these terrible things? It is *BAD* to be so competitive!" Generally in these cases what we are doing is identifying ourselves with one part of our chart at the expense of another (often major) part. The part we identify with and want to be like is often that part our parents or society approved of as "good," and the part of ourselves we disown is what our parents told us was "bad." Cultural conditioning plays its part too . . . in our culture, it is considered "bad" or "unnatural" if a man shows strongly Venusian characteristics. Actually a strong Venus in a man's chart is neither good nor bad, but only his nature.

The side of us our parents approved of is often reflected in our rising sign or ascendant. The ascendant shows our ways of trying to get along with others—our *front* or our tools for getting along in the world. The ascendant is *not* our essential self . . . the Sun and Moon are far more basic to our character. It is dismaying to me how many people are totally identified with their ascendant. A terribly meek double Leo friend—Sun *and* Moon in Leo—was much more receptive to astrology once she found out she had Pisces rising. "I always thought I was much more like a Pisces. Why, Leos aren't *nice* people!" A *double* Leo who shows none of that Leo at all is a Leo in a heck of a lot of trouble. I call that kind of trouble "getting trapped in your ascendant."

A client who was trapped in her ascendant was a Gemini with Sun conjunct both Uranus and Saturn. She had Cancer rising, and this was what most people saw of her—mother to the world. When I pointed out to her that she really didn't have a motherly bone in her body, she admitted that she really resents having to take care of all those people. "But it's BAD to be the way you described my Sun!" It took her a long time to accept that not only was it not *bad* for her to be her Sun, it was more real and more truly herself. I told her I felt she was brilliant, that she was wasting a lot of time mothering people who did not in the least appreciate being mothered, and that she would do a lot more for mankind in the end if she concentrated on developing the tremendous potential of her Sun.

Much self-hatred, then, can come about when the basic natures of your Sun and Moon or Ascendant are in disagreement. Another source can be hard aspects like squares or oppositions. A square, in particular, demands a resolution of the conflict within, and all too often a phony resolution comes about by identifying with one of the planets in the square against the other. Which side of the square you will take is somewhat unpredictable, possibly depending on the relative strengths of the two planets. The other side will also come out, however, perhaps in a disguised or unconscious manner that causes you to undo what you are consciously working toward.

Let us take, as an example, two people who have Mars square Neptune. The conflict may be "resolved" in two different ways, depending on their upbringing. A person, brought up in a deeply religious home where the child's natural competitiveness and aggression are regarded as "bad" may suppress open competition and compete in religious fanaticism—becoming a "holier than thou" type or an evangelist, for what is evangelism but a disguised lust for conquest? The other person with Mars square Neptune may have been brought up in a home which was terribly competitive and ridiculed compassion and spirituality, and may resolve the conflict by making a religion out of war and patriotism. Note how in both cases a strong hint of the suppressed planet comes through in a disguised way. A suppressed (in technical terms, *repressed*) planet is still very active, on the unconscious level, where it can often work in an unhealthy and self-defeating way. There are healthy ways of resolving the Mars-Neptune conflict, but not by ganging up on one of them and glorifying the other.

When you have two planets in conflict with each other or your Sun or Moon clashes with your ascendant, what can you do? Well, first stop making value judgements! The two things in conflict are both valid parts of yourself. They are neither intrinsically good nor bad, they just *are*. In order to find health and a degree of comfort, you must be fully aware of the needs and drives represented by both sides of the conflict and find some ways for both of them to be satisfied. For instance, I once did a chart reading for a woman with Sun in Capricorn and Moon in Aquarius. She had enormous responsibilities and drove herself to exhaustion, never taking vacations. Meanwhile, her Moon in Aquarius yearned for freedom—to break away, to do kinky things, to get rid of all those responsibilities. The conflict was beginning to affect her health. I explained all this to her, and, partly in jest, I wrote a realistic looking prescription: "Rx:

One free weekend a month, getting away from it all." She was so relieved at getting permission to take care of her own needs that she framed it and now faithfully refills her prescription once a month.

By becoming familiar with all the parts of your chart you will know yourself better. Recognize that each of the symbols in the chart represents a valid part of you that exists and must find an expression. Repressing or pushing aside some part of yourself is only asking for trouble—emotional or physical trouble or else "trouble" from the outside world that you bring on yourself. Remember that any repressed part of yourself will find expression in disguised, unconscious ways that may be unhealthy for you. Perhaps it will help you to accept yourself better if you get to understand the positive side of each planet, sign, house, and aspect. Your Mars in Scorpio in the third may lack tact, but you can work on that—what it does do is give you a very keen, analytical mind. . . a precious gift, for sure.

Some self-*dislike* can be valid. . . if you are expressing only the negative side of something in your chart. But disliking something about yourself and then going to work on it is a much healthier response than brooding on something and letting it grow to self-hatred. Self-hate and guilt are immobilizing and non-productive. Working toward a positive level of expression of your chart and its difficult points will change your image of yourself, and your self-love will grow. Realize, however, that we can exist at many different levels of functioning at the same time. Some of us may develop more quickly in the mental areas (Mercury, Uranus) than in the emotional areas (Moon, Neptune), while others might develop more fully in the relationship areas (Venus) first. Therefore, it doesn't make sense to judge ourselves harshly or to compare ourselves to others. We should also understand that it is unrealistic to expect perfections, and that it is very human to regress (go backwards) a little in times of stress in order to restabilize and to recharge before taking another forward step for growth.

Another source of self-hatred lies in faulty definitions. It is the old joke: "He says I'm stingy; I say I'm a good manager"... only in reverse. We define ourselves, often, in very negative and uncharitable ways... not seeing that the very things we see as weaknesses, others may see as strengths. The oyster, for all we know, may regard that pearl as a hideous deformity, while we regard it as a precious jewel. Likewise, a person with Mercury in Taurus may regard it as a defect that her thinking is very concrete... others may consider her quite refreshingly down to earth and sensible. It's all in your definitions of yourself. That's why it can be quite helpful, even for an advanced student of astrology, to have your chart done several times by others who may be able to give different perspectives on you and foster a more positive self-definition.

Take a long view of things also. The qualities that start off as weaknesses often develop into tremendous strengths, as we try so hard to compensate for them. (This is often the case with the house and sign your Saturn falls in.) You need to periodically re-define yourself. By hard work, you may have already overcome some of the weaknesses you are still feeling inferior about. Let your consciousness catch up with your growth. Or, you may still be in the process—we are always in process—of overcoming some of them, but at least see where you are in that process and how far you've come.

Other parts of ourselves that we regard as weaknesses are merely the consequences of specialization. The more time and energy you devote to any one thing, the less you have for something else, purely as a matter of course. I feel badly sometimes that I can't paint or draw, but I paint and draw with words, because that is where I have chosen to specialize. People with a stellium (a group of three or more planets) in one sign or house, or with Sun and Moon in one sign or house, or who have most of their planets in one quadrant of the chart, are especially prone to over-specialization. If you have a chart like this, you will find a great deal of your energy concentrated in one area of life.

Naturally, you will develop more skill and ability in that area of concentration and may consequently be lacking in other areas our culture may define as desirable or important. But why hate yourself for those lacks? Only by some degree of specialization and devotion can you build something really worthwhile. Many of the greatest talents of our time are one-sided people because they devote so much time to practicing their art. But to hate themselves for being one-sided? That's as silly as a great neurosurgeon hating himself because he can't pull teeth.

Self-hatred can also be a rather strange inversion of self-love. "Look at me! I'm so TERRIBLE! I'm the biggest monster on earth!" How very important that makes you, doesn't it? Neptunians often fall into this pattern—or Pisces-Leo combinations like my "meek" double Leo friend, who loved to dramatize her own sense of worthlessness. I asked a question in a poem once, and I still think it's a good one: "Why is true humility so foreign to the self-hating?" Find some other way of being important besides being miserable.

If you behave in self-defeating ways, start now to overcome these crippling patterns. In some cases, psychotherapy may be needed, but begin by understanding your natal chart in depth. It is a priceless tool for gaining perspective on the self, for finding the roots of conflict and self-defeat within us. By discovering the sources of self-defeat and self-hatred in your chart, you will be able to free the life-affirming parts to work more openly. Only by accepting all parts of yourself and allowing them positive expression can you become a healthy, fully-integrated person.

PART TWO
THE PLANETS &
THEIR FUNCTIONS

CHAPTER 2
THE SUN — CENTER OF OUR BEING

Popular astrology deals with Sun signs, and it is very chic among astrologers to put down any exploration of the zodiac as "Sun Sign Astrology." Astrologers are both right *and* wrong in doing this—*right* in that the complete natal chart must be drawn up for a true understanding of the individual and *wrong* in belittling the importance of the Sun. Just as the Sun is the center of our solar system from which all life in this system has evolved, so is the Sun in our charts the center of our being and the origin of our own life force. The sign of the zodiac it is in is crucial in forming your character and tells a great deal about you. Although we will not be exploring the Sun signs here, we well devote much time to understanding the role the Sun plays in our lives.

The Sun as a Celestial Body

If we look at the facts about our Sun, we gain support for the assertion that it is the most important factor in our charts. The Sun contains 99.9% of all matter in the solar system—the planets, their moons, the asteroids, comets, and meteors all together comprise only .1%.[1] The weight of the Sun is 700 times greater than the combined weights of all the planets.[2] Thus the sheer immensity of the Sun dwarfs any other part of the solar system, and the Sun in our chart represents that immense influence.

There could be no life without the Sun, and there could be no Sun without hydrogen. Hydrogen is the basic material of the universe, out of which stars such as our Sun are formed. Other matter is then produced by nuclear reactions going on inside the star. Incredibly high temperatures fuse hydrogen first into helium and then into increasingly more complicated elements. Hydrogen and helium comprise

---

1. Meir H. Degani, *Astronomy Made Simple*, Made Simple Books, 1963 edition.
2. Robert Jastrow, *Red Giants and White Dwarfs*, Signet Books, 1969. The book is both fascinating and inspiring. For someone like myself, with no real science background, it is also fairly easy to read.

99% of all matter (Jastrow, p. 42), and the process of changing hydrogen into helium takes up 99% of the lifetime of a star, while the remaining elements are formed in the last 1% of its life (Jastrow, p. 53).

It is clear that hydrogen is the basic matter out of which all other matter is formed. It is the simplest of all atoms, a single electron circling a nucleus of one neutron and one proton. I found a diagram of a hydrogen atom and was stunned to see that it looks exactly like the glyph for the Sun: ⊙ . Significantly, scientists designate hydrogen element *No. 1* and place it centrally in the table of elements, just as numerology assigns the number *1* to the Sun.[3] Burning hydrogen is what keeps the Sun alive, and billions of years from now when its hydrogen is all gone it will collapse in on itself and die. The Sun's heat and light gained from burning hydrogen are what keep us alive.

The Sun itself is alive, according to occultists like Vera Stanley Alder (the most readable of the lot). They teach that the stars and planets are living beings, evolved to an extent we cannot conceive of. Most scientists regard occultists as bizarre, yet the borderlines of modern physics and astronomy are steadily moving toward something mystical.[4] Consider this astronomer's words:

> The stars seem immutable, but they are not. They are born, evolve and die like living organisms. . . The elements of which our bodies are formed were manufactured. . . in the interiors of stars now deceased, and distributed to space when those stars exploded. . . If the sun explodes, at the end of its life, the planets will be consumed and their substance once more distributed into space, to be reincarnated in another solar system as yet unknown. (Jastrow, pp. 50 & 66.)

The book just quoted, *Red Giants and White Dwarfs*, has a theme germane to our search for the Sun's role in our

---

3. Here and in a number of other places in the book, you will find references to numerology. Numerology is not a major area of study for me, as I find greater depth in astrology. However, I am very interested in the cross-connections between astrology and other spiritual disciplines such as numerology because they tend to validate my knowledge. Where such cross-connections are known to me and seem germane, they will be remarked upon.

4. Appendix D in Lawrence LaShan's fascinating book *The Medium, the Mystic, and the Physicist* contains a table of statements by scientists and mystics, and it's hard to tell which is which. (Ballantine Books, 1966, pp. 253ff.)

lives. This theme is that all systems—from single atoms to cells to solar systems to entire galaxies—are organized in the same way. There is a center or nucleus around which all other matter in the system revolves. This principle is shown clearly in the ancient symbol for the Sun, ☉ , which proves to be a timeless diagram for understanding all of life. It strikes me that when the Bible says that God made man in His own image, it may not be talking about a man-shaped God at all, but only the fact that all life operates out of this same principle of matter revolving around a nucleus, including the atoms and cells that make up the human body.

If all things in life revolve around their center, so must we. In order to live fully and develop our best potential, we must be centered. To be centered is to act out of the innermost depths of our being, out of a sure and comfortable knowledge of who we are. Just as the Sun is the center of the solar system, the Sun in our charts symbolizes our personal center. Studying its sign, house and aspects can help us find ourselves. Ignoring the Sun in your chart, as so many astrologers seem to do, is risking the loss of that center around which everything in our lives must revolve. A good centering technique is to meditate on the Sun symbol itself, focusing on it until you feel yourself drawing deep inside. It is like a simplified mandala: ☉ . (The potent symbol for the Sun will have a section all its own, but I seem to be unable to talk about the Sun at all without referring to it.)

To be centered is not the same as being self-centered, as many people with prominent Sun or Leo placements can be. When we are children, we believe that everything revolves around us. We exist in a state psychologists call "infantile omnipotence." That is, we believe ourselves to be the center of our universe, that we create everything that comes to us, and that everything exists only for us. In short, we believe we are God. Actually, we ARE God, but so is everything else in the universe. (The Sun rules Leo, and Leos often retain for life this childish belief that everything revolves around them.)

The Sun remains the center of our solar system because of gravity. The force of gravity is the weakest of the forces holding our universe together, yet the Sun's gravity is so strong (28 times that of the earth) that it keeps all the planets in orbit around it (Jastrow, p. 38). Every planet in our chart also orbits around our own Sun, and its indrawing force should keep the Sun the center of our lives, rather than let one of the other planets take over. To be centered elsewhere than in your Sun or to let one of the planets assume more importance than the Sun leads us to become eccentric (literally, off-center) or self-defeating.

We can gain some insight by thinking about the phenomena associated with the Sun. Eclipses were greatly feared in antiquity; today nobody much is afraid of them except those astrologers who still see them as "afflictions" of great portent. (I'm sure eclipses do have an effect on the chart, but it has yet to be explained to me satisfactorily.) Since solar eclipses occur in predictable series of 2-5 a year, astronomers prepare well in advance and travel to places where the eclipse will be total. During a solar eclipse, they gain a great deal of information about the Sun's atmosphere and composition. The Sun in our charts represents both the ego and the basic self, and just as it takes an eclipse to show us the true nature of the Sun, we often learn most about our own true nature in times of stress when the ego is temporarily darkened or shut out.

Sunspots are another interesting phenomenon which seems to occur in regular cycles. The sunspot is a dark area that crosses the face of the Sun and creates magnetic storms on the earth. Astrologer Robert Knight explained sunspots to me by likening them to pimples on the Sun's surface—places where the Sun's grainy surface parts and material protrudes from underneath. This analogy interested me because metaphysically skin disturbances represent identity problems, and we get the most pimples as teenagers, when we are least sure of who we are. The Sun in our charts represents our basic identity.

This exploration of the Sun as a celestial body should demonstrate that it is by far the most potent force in the solar system and in our charts. As stars go, the Sun may be rather small and faint, but we couldn't exist without it. The Sun is the only real source of light in our solar system; the light of the planets is only reflected sunlight. If you want to find the true source of light in your own life, focus and meditate on the Sun in your chart.

The Sun Glyph & Its Power

The glyph for the Sun ⊙ is the most powerful of all astrological symbols and the richest in meaning. I teach astrology in a center for the treatment of alcoholism, and I once devoted an entire session to this symbol. We kept pushing deeper and deeper to see what lessons we could learn from the form and shape of it, and we finally reached such a profound level of understanding that several of the men were moved to tears. I only hope I can recapture some of the spirit of that session with you.

While I've always felt that the astrological symbols were very old, I recently found out that the symbol for the Sun is at least 50,000 years old and most likely a great deal older than that.[5] The evidence for this comes from tablets discovered in Mexico by archaeologists, who place the tablets in the tertiary geological era because of the conditions which surround them. On the tablets, the symbol ⊙ stood for the Sun, which was worshipped as a God named *Ra*. In later tablets, the symbol also represented the king; powerful kings were given the title *Ra* and regarded as divine. This equation of the king with the Sun/Godhead is seen in many countries and many eras—in the Egyptian Pharaohs, in the Sun kings of China, and in the European concept of the divine right of kings. In astrology, the Sun rules the regal sign, Leo. Interestingly, the outer layer of the Sun is called the corona (Latin for crown) because of its crown-like protrusions.

---

5. Hans Stefan Santesson, *Understanding MU*, Paperback Library, N.Y., 1970, p. 51.

In occult symbolism, the circle is said to represent totality, infinity, eternity, all there is. The dot in the middle of the Sun symbol ⊙ indicates a specific point, place, individual, or time within that totality. Yet it is never true totality, because there is always something greater. For instance, ⊙ could be an atom, the dot being the nucleus. If you were an electron, that atom would seem to stretch to infinity. Yet ⊙ could also represent a cell; from the nucleus, it would seem to stretch to infinity, yet there are millions of cells in one human being. From the point of view of a human being the solar system ⊙ seems to stretch to infinity, yet there are about 100 billion solar systems in our galaxy, which is so vast that the Sun takes 200 million years to rotate around the galaxy's center. Galaxies are not even the outer limits, because they occur in clusters of up to 10,000 and are probably revolving around some vast undiscovered center (Jastrow, pp. 18, 25, 33).

Since (in addition to all the systems traced above) the Sun represents the self in the chart ⊙ , it is both a symbolic confirmation that we are part of all that is, and it is *also* a pointed reminder that there are far greater things in the universe. We are divine, yet miniscule. We are separate, yet we are one with everything there is. However, for the person who is totally self-centered, that circle represents a wall between the self and all that is, a separation from the oneness. In astrological symbolism, the circle is also said to represent spirit. The dot in the circle is the center of our being, the soul, so the Sun symbol ⊙ reminds us that we are spiritual at the core of our being. The dot is surrounded by spirit, and God is all around us. The circle is a boundary or ring that keeps us from getting lost, and we can never escape our spirituality.

Leaving behind traditional symbolism and letting my intuition go to work, the symbol for the Sun also suggests an egg to me ⊙ . The egg is another source of life force out of which something develops. The egg is dormant, yet once fertilized contains all that is needed to produce an adult of a particular species. Thus the egg represents the total potential of an individual and so does the Sun in the chart. Our oneness with all life is shown by the course of development of the human embryo, for it goes through stages of looking like an amoeba, a fish, a reptile and a bird before it passes into an irrevocably human form at about seven weeks. A further confirmation of the relationship of the Sun symbol to the source of human life was revealed to me when I attended a feminist class on the female body. By arranging a plastic speculum, mirror, and flashlight, I was able to see my own cervix (the mouth of the womb). It resembled a bright red doughnut, and the shape was exactly like the symbol for the Sun!

The symbol also makes me think of a target with a bull's-eye, and the Sun in our charts is what we aim for. This is another reminder that we must focus and center ourselves if we want to hit the target. (It is also like looking down into a funnel or tunnel, both of which require concentration to remain in the center.) Besides a bull's-eye, the Sun symbol ⊙ looks like the human eye. The eyes are said to be the windows of the soul, and they are very revealing of the person's true character and intent. Likewise the Sun in the chart shows the soul and the true character. It looks like an eye, and the Sun in the chart is the *I*—both the I AM and the ego. The ego can get in the way of real self-development. If you are too self-centered, you lose sight of the spiritual center, the I AM.

The symbol ⊙ also reminds me of a rapidly spinning wheel. The Wheel of Fortune and the Wheel of Incarnations (Maya) immediately come to mind. The circle in the symbol says that all of life is cyclical and history is always repeating itself. The dot in the center shows that the only way to get off the wheel is to become centered in spirit. I believe that the sign, house, and aspects of the Sun in the chart show the most important tasks and goals of this soul in this particular incarnation and the place where the greatest development can occur.

As you can see, the Sun symbol is extremely rich in meaning. Once more, I suspect that what we've discerned is not the totality, but only the egg. If you keep meditating on this symbol, I'm sure even deeper levels of meaning will unfold.

CHAPTER 3

UNDERSTANDING THE MOON — REFLECTIONS ON DIANA

Is there any object in the sky more beautiful and fascinating than the Moon? It was an object of worship to primitive people all over the world who were in touch with the influence of the Moon's phases on the earth and its creatures. Recently some of the "superstitions" about the Moon have become respectable, as scientists, sociologists, and policemen discover their validity. In astrology, too, we recognize the great influence of the Moon on the individual, whether it be through gravity, something mystical, or as yet unknown. In Western astrology, the Moon is considered next to the Sun in shaping our character; in Indian astrology, it is given even greater weight than the Sun.

Moon Symbolism, Moon Worship & Women

The symbol for the Moon in astrology and other areas of the occult is the most recognizable of any: ☽ . But have you given any thought to why that particular phase of the moon (the waxing crescent) was chosen? Why not ☽ , ☺ , ☽ , or ☾ ? In her fascinating book, *Women's Mysteries*, Esther Harding says it is because the Moon meant growth and fertility to the ancients, and the waxing crescent was the phase at which the Moon had the most room to grow.[1] In addition, the New Moon proved to be the best time to plant crops, producing the most growth.

If you let your imagination and intuition flow freely when dealing with a pictorial symbol, you can tap into additional meanings the symbol may convey. For instance, I once noticed that a radar screen is shaped like the symbol for the Moon: ☽ . In selecting that shape for radar, the scientists unknowingly made use of a truth about one of the functions of the Moon in our lives. It does act like a radar screen, scanning, receiving and responding unconsciously to subtle impressions received from the outside

---

1. M. Esther Harding, *Women's Mysteries*, Harper, 1971.

world. This sensitivity and responsiveness is much of what gives Moon-ruled people (those with a strong Moon or planets in Cancer) their reputed intuition. Another lunar image is provided by astrologer Rod Chase, who points out that boats ☽ are shaped like the Moon. Boats hold and protect us—and protectiveness is a function of the Moon. The Moon, however, also rules the emotions, and Rod feels the Moon/boat similarity teaches us that the only way to deal with our emotions is to float on them rather than be swallowed up and drown in them.

Symbolism based on the Moon is present in many occult studies.[2] In ancient mythology the Moon goddess was Diana, who ruled over nature and fertility. Women who wanted children made offerings to her, as did pregnant women, who believed Diana would grant an easy childbirth. She was a very important goddess, and, as we can see, she ruled critical maternal functions. Knowing these beliefs from astrology and mythology, I was still surprised by a discovery I made while doing the progressions on my natal horoscope. Both times the Moon has made aspects by solar arc to my ascendant or midheaven, a crucial woman has come into my life—and both times the woman was named Diana!

Numerologists believe that the numeral 2 comes from the symbol for the Moon ♌ . The meaning of 2 in numerology is fairly similiar to some of the meanings of the Moon —it is the feminine principle, cooperation, and the helpmate. 2 is emotional and intuitive, just as is the Moon in astrology. When you break the name Diana down numerologically, it adds up to a 2. That can't be a coincidence. I also found a Moon-type hexagram in the *I Ching*. Its name is *The Receptive*, and it is made up of all Yin (feminine) lines. This hexagram denotes devotion, complementarity and the female-eternal principle. Significantly, this is hexagram number 2! The Moon and the Number 2 are also represented in the Tarot. If you put the twos of all four suits together, they seem to express variations of the cooperation-helpmate theme. . . or the lack of it. The number two Major Arcana is

---

2. These occult correlations to the Moon are taken from my article, "Reflections on Diana," *Your Personal Astrology*, 1/74. Reprinted with permission of Sterling Publications © 1974.

the High Priestess, who seems to be related to Diana. This card shows a deeply psychic and mysterious woman, schooled in ancient occult wisdom such as Wicca. The crescent Moon is at her feet, and she sits between two pillars representing good and evil.

Thus, we see that the Moon has a great deal of occult meaning. The book mentioned earlier, *Women's Mysteries*, is an extremely important one, not only for understanding the Moon and its mystical significance, but also for understanding the feminine part of our humanness—whether we be biologically male or female in this lifetime. The book traces the spontaneous and separate growth of the Moon religions in all parts of the world and how those religions grew and changed as culture evolved. It also shows how, in all these religions, the Moon was thought to be feminine and to have special importance to women. (In another important book, *The First Sex*, Elizabeth Davies demonstrates how the Moon religions took hold during ancient times when there was a matriarchy, and how the Sun-worshipping religions did not take hold until the patriarchy was established.[3]).

After reading *Women's Mysteries* and being captivated by it, I tried an experiment with one of my astrology classes, a group of recovering alcoholics at a treatment center in the Bedford Stuyvesant area of Brooklyn. I asked them to pretend they were an extremely primitive and isolated tribe meeting for the purpose of establishing a religion. They entered deeply into the experiment, assigning themselves roles in the tribe and discarding all knowledge that a primitive person could not gain from observations of nature. Startlingly, the results of their reasoning match the thinking of primitive people as outlined in the book. They independently decided to worship the Sun and Moon, both of which they had no control over and which were felt to be alive because they moved. The Sun was felt to be male, as it was stronger and more dominant. The Moon was unanimously regarded as female because of its softness, romantic

3. Elizabeth Davies, *The First Sex*, Penguin Books, 1972.

nature, and its constant changes. The growth of the Moon and its phases were likened to pregnancy in women and to the monthly menstrual cycle.

Rather than rebel at the seeming sexism of my class and of the book assigning the Moon to women and femininity, as I once would have, I was forced to conclude that there was something to it. However, since the Moon is, as we will see, an extremely dominant planet in the horoscope, what role should we assign to it in a man's chart? Some astrologers dismiss the Moon in a man's chart as representing the woman in his life. But the Moon rules such key functions as emotions and dependency needs—and it is unhealthy for a man to ignore either of these. Both exist in men fully as much as in women, but our culture has forced men to repress them—and, overall, I'd say that's pretty hard on a man. It is better to accept the Moon as being the feminine side of a man's psyche (the anima, in Jungian terms), just as Mars represents some of the so-called "masculine" strivings in a woman's chart. *Women's Mysteries* has a great deal to say about the male/female dichotomy and how we cannot be whole until we integrate both within us.

The Moon & Mothering
What You Give=What You Got

Perhaps the most crucial human function described by the Moon is mothering—the mothering you give and the mothering you got. We'll see that the two are nearly inseparable. A less sexist word for this function is *nurturing*—after all, we can get caring, feeding, and loving from our fathers and other people as well as our mothers. As grownups, men hopefully do take care of others (friends and relatives, as well as children), and this is one of the functions of the Moon in a man's chart, although an often suppressed or disguised one in our culture. For most people locked in a traditional upbringing, however, the Moon functions were most often filled by the mother so the Moon in the chart may be read as the mother. The Moon describes how well we can take care of others, gratify their needs, and how well we can accept those same needs in ourselves. It shows how comfortable we are with dependency. Can we tolerate feeling dependent and actively go out to get those needs met? And, similarly, can we respond when others are dependent on us?

With a Moon in Cancer, for instance, dependency is strong. The person may be extremely dependent on others and show it; or, conversely, may hide their own dependency, consciously or unconsciously, by going all out to take care of others. The trap here is that this mother-to-the-world pose can leave the person drained and feeling even more dependent. A Moon in Aries person, on the other hand, places a high value on their own independence and has a very low tolerance for other people's dependency. It gets in the way of all those bright, shiny new things they want to achieve.

Psychology teaches us that our attitude toward dependency in ourselves and others comes directly from our parents, particularly our mothers. If the parent was able to deal with our dependency in a loving but balanced way—neither over-protective nor neglectful—then we will also be able to handle dependency appropriately. A Moon/Saturn or Moon in Capricorn person had a mother (or parents) who was dutiful but cold toward their needs and who pushed them to grow up too fast. A Moon/Neptune or Moon in Pisces person may have had a parent who was outwardly more sympathetic to their needs but who was oddly elusive when the chips were down. Both of these people might have the same problems in responding to others as their parents did.

Like it or not, we generally become the kind of parents our parents were. As psychologically aware people, we may vow to raise our children differently than we were raised. Nevertheless, when the children actually come along, we are often dismayed to find ourselves sounding and acting just like our own parents. Why is this? The Moon shows the patterns, habits, and memories from our earliest years, many of which are unconscious. We live what we learn, and one of the things we learn from our parents is how to be a parent. Since it is mainly unconscious, these patterns are difficult to put under rational control. Children who were abused, for instance, very often grow up to be abusive parents.

The Moon also rules your basic sense of security, which early parenting influences in a crucial but unconscious way. It is unconscious because it happens long before the infant is able to think in words. It comes from the way the infant is held, how it is fed, and how it is responded to when it cries—whether all these things are done with love, with anxiety, with indifference, or even with hostility. At that time in our lives, we are totally dependent on the parent for our very survival. Thus the type of parenting you get at this preverbal stage shapes your attitude toward the world you live in. Is it a safe place or a hostile one? Do you feel lovable? Do you feel wanted or barely tolerated? An analysis of the Moon in your chart will answer these questions. In the preverbal stage we either develop or fail to develop *basic trust,* according to the theories of psychoanalyst Erik Erikson. Basic trust means that we find the world and the people in it good and trustworthy. This stage has a very great effect on our ability to allow other people to be close to us and on our over-all orientation to life.

The person with Moon in Scorpio, for example, learned very early not to trust. The parent may have pretended concern and caring (even to the point of being over-protective), but there was often some other, less loving motivation behind it. Many times, the parent was manipulative and controlling, while pretending to have only the best interests of the child at heart. Thus, the child learned to be suspicious and, in self-defense, to try to second-guess others and find out their real motivation. As an adult, the person often adopts some of the parents' controlling patterns of behavior. In contrast, the person with Moon in Taurus, unless the Moon has difficult aspects, had more positive nurturing. The parents were stable and accepted the child's needs. They were more forthright, not so hard to understand or so emotional as with the Moon in Scorpio. As a result, the child grows up secure and feeling that he and the world are basically okay. (Naturally, other aspects in the chart can modify this.) Taurus is the sign traditionally thought to be the best placement for the Moon—its "exaltation." We always have to ask ourselves, "Best for what?" since Moon in Taurus has its drawbacks also, but for a sense of basic trust and security, it is a good sign.

Each person needs different things in order to feel secure, and the Moon in your chart shows the conditions under which you would feel most emotionally secure. A person with the Moon in the eleventh house would feel most secure when surrounded by friends or in some meaningful group. Someone with the Moon in the seventh usually only feels secure when involved in a long-term intimate relationship. The sign and house position can conflict —to have it in Aquarius means there is only security in freedom and change. The Moon in Aquarius in the fourth? Better invest in a mobile home. Many people may judge themselves harshly. For example, the Moon in Aquarius in the fourth person may say "It's bad for me to be so restless." Astrology can help you recognize those needs as valid and important and help you set out to meet them.

Generally, the Moon's sign, house, and aspects will describe your actual mother—to the extent that sometimes the child's Moon sign is the mother's Sun sign. What is interesting, however, is that children in the same family may have vastly different Moons. In one family, for instance, the older brother and sister both have Moon in Aries, but the younger sister has Moon in Scorpio. The older children were both encouraged to be independent (Aries), but at the time the younger sister was born, the mother nearly died. (Scorpio is sometimes associated with death.) For that reason, perhaps, the quality of the relationship between the mother and the younger sister was very different. She was pampered, overprotected, and called "Baby Doll" up to the time she was 14. We can speculate that the mother unconsciously resented that child bitterly for bringing her so close to death, but covered this feeling up by the overprotection and pampering. (This is one pattern you may find with Moon in Scorpio.)

Why do these discrepancies in Moons in the same family occur? What the Moon describes is not the actual mother, but the child's experience of her. That is, it doesn't show the mother as a total person separate from the child, but only the child's-eye view of her. Parents cannot treat all children alike—some children are better loved, some rub you the wrong way, some remind you of people you love or hate. Then, too, conditions in the home can change, and this can cause a difference in the mothering.

You can actually trace the history of a family through the sequence of Moons in the offspring. For instance, an early child or two may have Moon in Taurus, showing a warm and giving relationship with the mother. After the birth of a third child, however, perhaps economic conditions force the mother to go to work. Perhaps that child is born with Moon in Capricorn, showing that the mother is now more serious and intent on business, with less left over to give the child when the work day is finished. There are still similarities—both Taurus and Capricorn are earth signs—but the third child doesn't experience as much warmth from the mother, and isn't allowed to be a baby long enough. The mother pushes the child to grow up and be less of a burden on her, because she is worn out from working.

To take another example, sometimes a child with Moon in Libra (or other crucial placements in that sign) is conceived because the mother feels it will cement a marriage that is breaking apart (or, if not yet married, in the hope it will induce the man to marry her). This strategy rarely works out, because in reality a new baby puts a great stress on a relationship, even one that is working well. So, when the already-strained relationship breaks up or becomes more distant, the mother turns to her Moon in Libra child for the love and closeness she is missing from the child's father.

The child then grows up needing that kind of constant closeness and being strongly motivated to form relationships. This may be a person who can't stand to be alone—it makes him/her insecure and unhappy.

The Moon & Emotions

The Moon in our chart also shows our emotions and how we deal with them, as well as how we respond to the emotions of people around us. This, again, relates back to the nurturing we had as a very young child. How well our parents responded to our emotional expressions has a great deal to do with what emotions we allow ourselves to feel and how we deal with them and with other people's emotions.

In the case of people born with the Moon in an air sign (particularly Gemini and Aquarius, not so much Libra), the mother was often cold to the child's emotions and tended to detach herself from the child when it cried or expressed some other emotion the mother found unpleasant. As a result, the child learned to cut off all emotions and to be detached from them. . . it was either that or lose the mother's love and approval. In an extreme case, this can lead to a schizoid-type person, detached from all emotions. Often, with the air sign Moons, the mother could handle feelings only on an intellectual basis, asking the child to explain them away or make them rational. (But, then, there is little that is rational about our feelings.) As adults, these people intellectualize feelings rather than being in touch with them. They want to talk away their emotions and the emotions of other people. I've seen cases where imitative Moon in Gemini people know intellectually that people are "supposed" to have feelings about certain situations, so may counterfeit emotions that aren't really there in order to be more socially acceptable.

Earth sign Moons can also have a certain amount of difficulty in dealing with emotions. If you can't see it, touch it, or taste it, it ain't real. Moon in Capricorn and

Virgo want to analyse those "irrational" feelings away. Moon in Taurus is more accepting of emotions and of nearly everything else, but will work hard to restore serenity. The primary emotion Moon in Capricorn or Virgo people allow themselves is melancholic self-recrimination over their lack of perfection—an emotion that arises directly from their parents, who were over-critical. Nonetheless, earth sign Moons approach emotions on a practical level—trying to find out what's causing the problem and what concrete steps can be taken to alleviate it. For that reason, they can be a Rock of Gibraltar to others who are going through an internal emotional crisis and who, as a result, are having difficulty dealing with the demands of the outside world.

Fire sign Moons (Aries, Leo, Sagittarius) respond more actively and even aggressively to most situations that confront them in life, and that goes for emotions too. They instinctively mobilize to stop the thing that's bothering them or to go after the thing they need. Anger is an emotion most of us have trouble dealing with, but here the fire sign Moons are better off than most, unless there are difficult aspects from planets like Saturn, Pluto, or Neptune. The main lack I find in the fire sign Moons is sensitivity to other people's feelings. They are so gung ho about doing their own thing that they don't readily slow down to consider how you might feel about their actions. You first have to get their attention. Then, if you are somehow identified as being part of them (typical of Aries or Leo) or if their ego gets involved, they will respond to your emotions the same way they'd respond to their own—"Charge!"

Water, in occult studies, refers to emotions, and the water sign Moons are the most emotional of all. Some unsympathetic souls even say they revel in it. With Moon in Cancer or Scorpio, a considerable amount of energy is invested in discovering, experiencing, and digesting emotions. Paradoxically, Moon in Pisces, which is potentially the most emotional, constantly attempts to escape from unpleasant feelings, leading in some cases to an addictive personality or to living in a fantasy world. Water sign Moons are also very sensitive and responsive to other people's feelings. Often, on an intuitive level, they feel what you feel. The primary difficulty with water sign Moons is getting so hung up in their emotions that they lose some effectiveness in dealing with the outside world. With emotions, as with most other things in life, we need to strike a balance.

To conclude, the Moon in our birth charts has a very great significance, and the fourth house, which is connected with the Moon, rules roots and foundations. If the Moon in your chart is placed in a difficult sign or receives difficult aspects, then something went wrong in laying the foundations or establishing roots. In such a case, dependency and the ability to trust are deeply affected, and you may also have difficulty in dealing with emotions in a balanced way. Thus, getting a good understanding of the Moon in a chart is extremely important.

CHAPTER 4
MERCURY & THE MIND

Mercury is the planet governing mental skills, intelligence, verbal abilities, and communication. People with Mercury or Gemini strong in their charts often excel in mental tasks and can charm us with wit and an engaging line. But Mercury can also be slick and superficial, and popular astrology warns us, "Don't rely on Gemini." In its proper place, though, intellect is a great tool. Let's see if we can find some clues as to what that proper place should be.

Like our Moon, Mercury has no atmosphere due to the gravitational pull of its nearby parent (the Sun). Also like our Moon, it has phases; with the proper telescope, you can see a New, Crescent, Half and Full Mercury. This suggests that the proper place of Mercury (intellect) is as a satellite to the Sun, which is our basic character or soul.* Intellect and verbal ability are valuable only when in proper balance to the rest of the character and the body. The Sun is the heart, and words and learning are empty and mechanical unless you also have heart. Mercury is tiny compared to the Sun, and intellect is only a small part of the total being. The Sun, not Mercury, is the center of the solar system, and we cannot make the mind the center of our lives without becoming eccentric, which literally means off-center.

Mercury stands between Venus and the Sun in our solar system, and Mercury (communication) is the bridge between our inner selves (Sun) and the other people we want to share with (Venus). Mercury always stays close to the Sun in the zodiac, but if our thoughts are too wrapped up in ourselves, we create a barrier instead of a bridge. It is interesting how much the symbols for Mercury ☿ and Venus ♀ look alike—Venus rules love, and it is hard to sustain an intimate relationship if you can't communicate with the person.

---

*Eleanor Bach was perhaps the first astrologer to note how the physical characteristics of a planet matched the astrological function. Some duplication of her ideas in the following chapters is inevitable.

Mercury — Myth, Mirth, Metal & Medicine

In mythology, Mercury was the messenger of the gods, a speedy guy with wings on his cap and shoes. It is said that thoughts have wings, and our thoughts and words do move swiftly carrying our messages. Mercury was also the god of commerce and industry, and we cannot carry on business without communicating. Often, however, what advertising and sales people are communicating isn't the whole truth but that version of the truth which will sway us. Likewise, the god Mercury was so cunning and clever that thieves of antiquity adopted him as their patron saint. Mercury's tools, words, are as often used to cover up and deceive as they are to exchange and communicate. Mercurial people, too, are often amoral in the use of their skill with words.

Besides being a planet in our solar system and a myth-ological god, mercury is a metal, and a very peculiar one at that. It is liquid in form, yet doesn't really behave like water. If you pour it out on a table, it won't leave any traces of wetness. Instead, it forms into little silvery balls and runs off in all directions. Because of its sensitivity to changes in temperature and pressure, mercury is used in thermometers and barometers and in taking blood pressure. Mercurial people, too, are paradoxical and similar to the metal in many ways. Fluid, adaptable, and changeable, they respond easily and quickly to the changes in the social climate around them. They can appear quite sensitive and responsive to other people, yet it is a very different kind of sensitivity than you find in the water signs. (In astrology and other occult sciences, water stands for feelings.) Mercurial sensi-tivity consists mainly of perceiving and comprehending things with the intellect rather than with the emotions, which mercurial people sometimes tend to run away from in all directions rather than face. However, this ability for detachment that is found in mercurial individuals is also what keeps us from drowning in emotions, helping us keep a rational perspective on our more irrational fears and feelings. In a counseling or therapy situation, particularly, a strong Mercury focus is essential, for without it we would lack the awareness, detachment, and insight that can result from verbal exchange.

Another common name for the metal mercury is quicksilver. Both *quicksilver* and *mercurial* are words that have been used to describe fast-moving, fast-talking, and ever-changing individuals. The metal runs off in all directions when you pour it, and Mercurians are restless and distractable, with a tendency to scatter themselves. But scattering doesn't hurt the metal mercury, nor does it seem to hurt mercurial people—they have the ability to bring all those scattered bits of data together and make connections between them, just as the droplets of mercury readily coalesce. Then, too, going off in all directions is one sure way not to get stuck in the mud! Mercury people get exposure to many different points of view and have a broader exposure to a variety of experiences and ideas than do most other people. As a result, they are interesting conversationalists and have a seemingly unlimited capacity for mental growth.

The metal mercury readily takes on the shape of the things it comes into contact with. Dip a dime in mercury and it adheres to all the little grooves and surfaces. Likewise Mercury people instinctively mimic others, whether consciously or unconsciously. This is true from the trivial level of doing humorous imitations to more profound levels of behavior and motivation. When they are with you, they take on your thinking and behavior, so that they seem as much like you and connected to you as your own identical twin (Gemini's symbol). However, when they leave you, the droplets of mercury coalesce and adhere to the surface of the next social contact. This tendency for mimicry, however, does give them the capacity for mixing well with all kinds of people and for adapting to all kinds of situations, rather than just being stuck in the cultural pattern they were born into.

Mercury is used extensively in switches and other electrical devices because it is a good conductor of electricity. It is the heaviest liquid in existence (13 times as heavy as water), but its fluidity creates less friction and resistance in the electron flow than do the solid metals. So, too, do the verbal skills and charm of Mercury people allow them to move fluidly around all different social circles without creating resistance and friction. The gift of gab, or blarney if you will, cuts down on the friction that differences of opinion or background might create. (Interestingly, Uranus, which rules electricity, is considered the higher octave of Mercury—i.e. what the planet Mercury would be if stepped up to its highest level.)

One of the most common uses of mercury is in medicine. It is used in mercurochrome and other disinfectants, in certain medicinal compounds, and in dental work; yet mercury and many of its compounds, are poisonous. The god Mercury, too, was connected with medicine in the eyes of the ancients. His staff, with its two curled serpents, is still used as a symbol for the medical profession. It has been said that laughter is the best medicine, and the planet Mercury is the astrological ruler of wit and humor. I recall reading the case of a gravely ill man who actually cured himself with laughter. The medicines and treatments prescribed for his illness, a rare one, were only making him steadily worse. He finally persuaded his doctor to discontinue them, and he stayed in the hospital but devoted several periods a day to reading or watching humorous material. Even when he didn't feel like it, he laughed and laughed and laughed. After a few weeks, he was significantly better. Repeatedly, blood tests taken before and after his laughing times showed a lowering of the level of toxic materials in his blood. Eventually, he returned to full health. Admittedly, this case is unusual, but it does suggest that the release of tension we enjoy when we have a good laugh can have a healthful physical effect.

The association of Mercury with humor is backed up by studying the charts of comedians. (If you're interested in pursuing this for yourself, many of today's popular comedians and other celebrities have their birthdates published in the *Information Please Almanac*.) Some of them have Sun, Moon, or rising sign in Gemini, but even more often, you'll find Mercury conjunct the Sun. To name just a few who have this conjunction, there are Woody Allen (Sun and Mercury in Sag), Bob Hope (Sun and Mercury in Gemini), Phyllis Diller (Cancer), Jack Paar (Taurus), Jimmy Durante (Aquarius), and Charles "Peanuts" Schulz (Sag). What is interesting is that the sign this Sun-Mercury conjunction is in then colors the humor or selects the target for satire. Aquarius is associated with splits and breaks, and Jimmy Durante said, "I don't split infinitives; when I goes to work on them, I breaks them in little pieces." Phyllis Diller is not the domestic type Cancer, she's the antithesis, but the point of her humor is her domestic struggles. Gemini rules current events and relatives, and Bob Hope kids a lot about both. All the signs and planets are said to rule parts of the body, and I'd have to say that Mercury rules the funny bone.

Communication & Intelligence

Mercury rules communication and intelligence, and the two are often taken as inseparable. The person who is glib with words is often estimated to be more intelligent than someone not so verbal who may be a deeper thinker. IQ tests are largely based on verbal ability, and the foreign born or otherwise language-deprived do not score well on IQ tests. There is lip service to the idea that IQ tests discriminate against certain kinds of people who are perfectly intelligent, but group IQ tests are still permitted to determine our school placement and thus to some extent the quality of our educational experience. In a similar way, we have always thought of monkeys, apes, and gorillas as far behind man in intelligence. There is a great deal of experimental work going on with these primates now, however, and the early results are surprising. When taught sign language or some other form of non-spoken communication, apes can have a large vocabulary and reason for themselves in ways similar to man. Some have even been given IQ tests and have scored at 75 or 80. The point researchers are making about this is that we didn't teach them to think or to communicate, as they did this with each other all along. We only taught them a means of communicating with man, and only when we did this were we able to appreciate the extent of their intelligence.[1]

Communication may be somewhat independent of intelligence, but without communication of some sort, we cannot make use of the intelligence of other people. Learning that comes from others' experience rather than our own cannot happen without it. Since the experience of any individual is necessarily less than the shared experience of the group or culture, the inability to communicate, read, and write rather limits the amount you can learn. Native intelligence can take you only so far, at least in the present century. A study of Mercury in individuals' birth charts can give us clues to how they learn best, but I'm not so sure it always shows us their intelligence or how it will be put to use. For example, I know of astrotwins born 8/26/50 who are quite different in intelligence. One was Robin Rogers, the Mongoloid daughter Dale Evans wrote about in *Angel Unawares*. The other is a young male student of mine who is quite bright but who is in treatment for alcoholism. The time of birth of Robin Rogers isn't known, and certainly that might help us to differentiate between the two charts, but the aspects to Mercury couldn't be that different.

The inability to communicate and the feeling of being misunderstood are miserable to live with, but like all skills they get better with practice. The alcohol treatment center

---

1. A fascinating review of the research appeared in the New York Sunday Times Magazine section on 6/12/77. It was "The Pursuit of Reason," by Harold T.P. Hayes, p. 21.

where I'm teaching astrology takes communication very seriously, because they know how handicapped their patients can be without it. One of the most intense class sessions we ever had was about Mercury. When I had presented the basic idea, the students got involved in a very heated discussion of the problems various class members had in communicating.

In order to analyse the problems an individual has in this area, you'd look at Mercury and its aspects and also the third house and any planets in it. For example, one of my students at the center has Mercury, Mars, and the Sun conjunct in Aquarius in the twelfth house. (No, he's not a comic! In fact, he seems to have no sense of humor at all— perhaps because the conjunction is in the twelfth.) He is bright, but has a great deal of trouble getting his ideas across. Then, too, he's a rebellious nonconformist who is angry with society for not living up to his ideals. His thoughts center on past injustices, and he's unable to look at the part he plays in his own troubles. Out of resentment and disappointment, he began drinking heavily. Now that he's in treatment, the positive side of that twelfth house combination can come out in helping him delve into his own unconscious and perhaps in eventually using his knowledge to help others.

The Positive Power of Thinking

Mercury rules words, ideas, and thoughts. The Bible says, "In the beginning was the word." It is talking about the creation of our universe, but the same process goes on whenever we create something. The idea comes first, then the actions which bring the idea into reality. I first thought of this book, this chapter, and this page and only then did they come into existence. A *concept* comes before a *conception.* If you accept this, the implications are profound. If ideas are what create our experience, then if your experiences are negative, it must be because your thoughts, beliefs, and concepts are negative also. So long as your thoughts dwell on the negative, the experiences you draw into your life will be negative too. If you say constantly, "No one can love me," then you shut yourself off to love and you won't find it. If you say before each job interview, "I know I won't be hired," then of course you won't be. Alcoholics can't stop drinking as long as they believe they can't. It is only when a new, positive idea enters their thoughts that they are able to stop. Thus, if you want to change the negative experiences in your life, you have to change the patterns of thought that are creating them. This is no simple task—so many of our beliefs and habits of thinking were drummed into us as children and continue to be reinforced as adults.

The helpfulness of teachings like Norman Vincent Peale's *Power of Positive Thinking* and Maxwell Maltz's *Psychocybernetics* is that they give us tools to use in working on those negative thought patterns. Both of these men were influenced by the New Thought Movement, which encompasses Religious Science, Science of Mind, and Unity. If you feel that neutralizing your negative thoughts and replacing them with positive ones would improve the quality of your life, I'd suggest you look into some of these ideas. (Interestingly, Mercury rules Gemini, and Norman Vincent Peale, who wrote *The Power of Positive Thinking*, was a Gemini, born 5/31/1898.)

Occult teachings say that there is a plane called the astral where we go during dreams, in trance, or after death. On the astral plane, our thoughts take immediate visible shape, although they are not of a material you can touch. When we "hold a thought" for a very long time, be it a positive or a negative one, then the astral thought form shapes the reality of that thought on the material or earthly plane. So, it is true that thoughts are things having power in themselves, and we must be careful what we are thinking. We can then understand in a new way what the Bible is getting at in the verse that says, "As a man thinketh, so he is."

CHAPTER 5
VENUS — LEARNING TO LOVE

During the time I was preparing this chapter, I was walking along the street and suddenly found a heart at my feet —a pretty, heart-shaped pendant with old-fashioned flowers. Love is like that. It doesn't do any good to work at finding it, to plot and scheme to get it, or to try all the tricks in the book to win it. You just go about the business of developing yourself, and one day it's there. It doesn't even have that much to do with deserving it—some of the most rotten and reprehensible philanderers have dozens of people in love with them. Venus is as capricious and elusive a planet as any in the solar system. Let's try to get some understanding of its role in our lives.

Venus and Jupiter are traditionally labelled "benefics" (good guys) by astrologers, yet both have their ill effects when misused. The negative Venusian can be lazy, self-indulgent, vain, and greedy. Certainly, Venusians can be charming and physically attractive, but if they allow themselves to fall back on those attributes to get through life, they fail to develop much of their potential or character. Many beautiful women have called their looks a curse—not that they get much sympathy from the rest of us, but beauty apparently can have its drawbacks.

Rod Chase has pointed out that Venus can be a trap that is a parody of true relating. He cites the *Venus* fly-trap and *venereal* disease (with Venus as its root-word) as indications that Venus has its perils. When we use beauty, charm, or wealth, to trap another person into loving us, that love will probably last only as long as the beauty or wealth it was based on. Yet among many men and women, these superficial Venusian traits are the basis for judging and accepting or rejecting potential partners. Likewise, viewing someone else as a sex object is another depersonalized way of relating. True equality, sharing, and loving cannot exist under any of these circumstances, and both you and your partner lose some of your humanity in doing so.

Part of my belief that Venus was originally regarded as a malefic comes out of the theories of Immanuel Velikovsky. (See, for example, *Worlds in Collision*, Pocket Books edition, 1977.) Velikovsky was one of the most respected scientists of the 1950's until he published his radical ideas about the origin of Venus. He felt that within recorded history Venus erupted as a comet out of the mass of Jupiter, and that before settling into its present orbit, it twice came within collision range of the earth and caused massive upheavals and destruction. Velikovsky attempted to give evidence for these ideas by an extremely brilliant reconstruction of historical data, but was ostracized by the scientific community. However, he also made certain predictions about the temperature, atmosphere, and rotation of Venus that were radically different from accepted beliefs. When subsequent space probes, including the landing on Venus, showed his predictions to be true and his theory the only possible explanation, Velikovsky once more began to be accepted by his peers. If his theories are correct, then Venus was not regarded by the ancients as a friendly force at all. Sacrifices and temples to Venus were originally meant to propitiate and keep the destruction from recurring. Only as Venus appeared to "hear" their prayers and settle into a stable and non-threatening orbit, did people come to regard it as a force of love.

I believe that the physical traits of each planet in our solar system are analogous to the planet's role in our lives. Velikovsky's history of Venus, to me, says that love (Venus) can be a destructive force in our lives until we learn to put it in its proper place—orbiting the Sun. The Sun represents our center, our I AM, and we cannot let love of another person become the center without becoming off-centered ourselves. If we do put another human being at the center and then lose that other human being, we are left with a vacuum or void. The balance between self and other is difficult to find. In fact, the conflicts represented by Venus can be just as hard to deal with as those represented by those awesome outer planets, Saturn, Uranus, Neptune or Pluto. By far the greatest number of letters I receive for my advice column have to do with love—lovers not getting along, lovers who have left (up to 25 years ago in some cases) and lack of love. Uniformly, these people are miserable. To love and to be loving in a balanced and healthy way without sacrificing our own individuality seems to me to be one of the most difficult lessons in life.

The Symbols for Venus & Libra

The glyph for Venus ♀ should be familiar because both the Women's Movement and the general public have chosen it to represent women. Actually, it's not such a liberated symbol—Venus has to do with some of the very things the Movement has disowned, such as a preoccupation with beauty, seductiveness, and bending over backwards to keep the peace. In mythology, Venus was the goddess of love, yet women now wish to be known as *persons* rather than love goddesses.

What does it teach us about our culture that Venus is so readily accepted as female? Venus represents the power of attractiveness, seductiveness, beauty, grace, sensuality, affection, cooperation, sympathy and art. All these characteristics of Venus, then, are considered the proper role for women. In this view, women can't go out actively to get what they want but should make themselves beautiful samples of "fascinating womanhood" to seduce their men into getting the things they want. All men have the planet Venus in their charts as well, but our culture suppresses these characteristics in men and labels them effeminate. Yet men have as much need as women do to live out their Venus directly, rather than vicariously through the women in their lives. We have to become aware that it is not astrology per se but our culturally-biased interpretation that labels Venus female.

Let's see what else the glyph for Venus may tell us about the planet. Many astrologers have noted that Venus is shaped like a flower—a beautiful, delicate perfumed object that we give as a token of love. Bulbs that are forced fail to flower again, and so does love that we try to force.

Rod Chase has even discovered a painting by Picasso called *LaFemme Fleur* (Woman-Flower), in which a woman with a head like a flower is shaped like the symbol for Venus. The glyph reminds us also of a looking glass ♀ , and Venusian people can be very concerned with their appearance and quite vain. Those with Venus conjunct the Sun or ascendant and many with Libra rising are often prone to narcissism. I used to think the line through the handle of the mirror showed someone hanging on to it, but now it occurs to me that perhaps it's a "forbidden to" sign like the ones we see now about smoking: ⊏══⟋══⬭. The crossbar on the mirror may be saying, "Don't be so vain, don't look at yourself so much; think of others." On the other hand, Venus without the crossbar looks like a lollipop, ♀ , and the crossbar might also be warning that you don't have to be a *sucker* in a relationship—nor should you suck the other person dry.

One of the symbols for Libra is the old-fashioned scale ⚖ on which both sides must be made to balance. Regardless of whether Libra is strong in your chart, an analysis of your Venus will tell you how you strive for balance. I personally have nothing in Libra, but my Venus is conjunct Uranus, the indicator of astrology, and I strive constantly for a balanced view of various factors in the horoscope. I also use astrology to keep my emotions and impulses in balance. The lack of planets in Libra, or having difficult aspects to Venus, can also indicate a problem in keeping your physical balance. I fall down rather a lot, and, with Venus conjunct Uranus, it is because my ankles suddenly give way. On the mental and spiritual levels as well, a lack of balance can be related to Venus/Libra deficits. On the other hand (a Libran expression!), balance is the Venus/Libra lesson for *all* of us to master. I've known numbers of Libras who were striving so desperately for balance that they became unbalanced. Being overweighted toward mental, emotional, relationship, or physical concerns leads to an unhealthy imbalance in our lives. Yet, who is to say whether some degree of overbalancing (specialization) might not be necessary for success?

I once discovered something interesting about the glyph for Libra: ♎ . I was trying to explain the laws of chance to a friend, and drew a picture of the "normal," or bell curve, which most statistical distributions fall into. A sample graph with this curve is shown here:

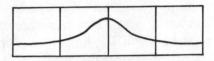

When you extract that curve from the graph, you get something which greatly resembles the glyph for Libra: ♎ . Let's look at the connections between the normal curve and the sign of Libra (♎). Blind justice and impartial fair play have been connected both with Libra and the game of chance called life. Keeping a balance, following the golden mean, and averaging things out, are Libra desires. Significantly, one of the first areas in which the normal curve was found, and where it is most often cited, was in scores on intelligence tests—and the sign Libra is much concerned with intelligence and intellectual pursuits. The connections, then, are significant, and I have trouble believing it came about by "pure chance." I believe that the designers (human or otherwise) of our astrological symbols incorporated a great deal of spiritual wisdom into them, if we will only let our intuition perceive it.

Venus in Exaltation, Detriment & Fall

Ordinarily, I do not pay a great deal of attention to the categories of exaltation, detriment, and fall for any planet, because I find they often work out in ways contrary to popular astrological belief. For the planet Venus, however, I find that thinking about these categories helps me to understand the nature of Venus and its proper role in our lives. (For readers unfamiliar with these terms, *exaltation* is the sign where a planet is supposedly at its best, *detriment* is a sign where the planet is ill at ease, and *fall* is a sign where the planet is supposedly at its weakest or worst.) Venus is in exaltation in Pisces, in fall in Virgo, and in detriment in Scorpio and Aries.

An image came to me when I was thinking very seriously about love relationships, which Venus rules. I got a flash of a couple slow-dancing and immediately could see the reason Venus is exalted in Pisces, the sign of the dance. An intimate relationship, such as marriage, should be like a dance. One partner is leading, but only nominally rather than in the sense of controlling. Each is keenly sensitive to the moves of the other, and each knows and does his part reciprocally. There is flow, ease, rhythm, and grace to the relatedness. Each knows when to go backwards or yield, in what Rod Chase calls the strategic retreat of Pisces. Later, I realized that this image is based on a rather old-fashioned idea. Both intimacy and dance have changed since the days of the two-step. In modern rock dancing, the couple do not lean on each other, and neither is leading. Both improvise and "do their own thing" and may or may not reflect their partner's motions, depending on how it suits them. There is freedom, equality, spontaneity, individuality, and creative self-expression in this kind of dance—and in the kind of marriage or close relationships our society is now evolving. However, Venus (and Libra, which it rules) is concerned with balance, and if the two dancing partners or two people involved in a relationship become too involved in their own thing, they risk losing contact with each other and may head in totally different directions (as happens in so many relationships these days). So, the key again is to find the right balance between contact (slow dancing) and self-expression (free-form dancing).

Venus is in fall in Virgo, and many negative things have been written about Venus in that sign. The sixth house, which Virgo is related to, provides an image to understand why. The sixth house rules servants, among other things, and if you are a servant to your loved one or he/she is a servant to you, there is no equality in the relationship and it therefore suffers. Venus is in detriment in both Scorpio and Aries, again, it seems to me, because the crucial factor of *equality* can easily be missing from such love relationships. An idea about the nature of Venus in Scorpio can be discovered in the traditional marriage ceremony. Marriage is supposedly related to Libra or the seventh house, but I have come to see lately that traditional marriage vows are extremely colored by Scorpio or the eighth house. The promise, *"to have and to hold,* in sickness and health, *for richer or poorer, until death do us part,"* is very much like the eighth house, in that the partner is seen as property to be owned—and the laws of our society are still not completely free of the ancient concept that the wife is chattel and cannot own and control her own property or her own life. If the loved one is owned and possessed, there is no equality, and Venus is in detriment. In our individualistic Aquarian age, many people are rejecting the old marriage vows and their implications and instead making up their own. There is also no equality when relatedness is something *done to* or *done for* the other person, in the sense of dominating or intruding on the other person's right of free choice or their freedom to grow along their own path. When Venus in Aries is expressed as a *doing to* kind of relatedness, I can see why Venus would be in fall there. Also, Venus in Aries represents a style that is very *action-oriented*, but this can be detrimental if the person becomes so wrapped up in *doing* things that there is seldom a pause to be receptive to other people.

I do believe, however, that each planet in each sign has its positive and its negative expression. For example, many humanitarians have Venus in Virgo—the love of service—and many healers have Venus in Scorpio—the healing power of love. Rather than putting down or praising any planet in any particular sign, you should try to put each planet and each aspect in your chart to work in its most positive form. Astrology is not meant to be used to put down and condemn people, but to uplift and enlighten them. That is why Uranus, the planet of astrology, is exalted in Scorpio, the sign of regeneration.

Venus & the Outer Planets — Problems in Personal Love

While difficult aspects between Venus and the inner planets can show problems in relating, they are nothing compared to the heartaches that can arise when Venus is in difficult aspect to the outer planets—Saturn, Uranus, Neptune, and Pluto. (By difficult aspects, I mean conjunctions, semisquares, squares, quincunxes, and oppositions. See the chapter on aspects.) I find the conjunctions to Venus the most difficult, but all such aspects can indicate trouble in forming relationships. Let's see how Venus is affected by the outer planets.

Venus and Saturn: The combinations of Venus and Saturn can be devastating to the person's ability to form relationships and to their feeling of being love-worthy. Generally one or both parents were Saturnian in the negative sense—rather cold, rigid, up-tight, somber, authoritarian and unable to show affection. Doubtlessly they saw the child mostly as an unwanted extra responsibility, an added burden, or even as coming in the way of their goals and ambitions. The parents could not love the playful, childish qualities of their offspring, so the child learned to grow up as rapidly as possible in order not to experience the parents' displeasure. The only way to please the parents was to be as Saturnian as *they* were, so the child learned that the only way to be "loved" is to be serious, business-like, reliable, responsible, successful. . . a model child.

The Venus-Saturn aspect can be so devastating because it contains what psychologists call a *double-bind* (a "damned if you do and damned if you don't" kind of set-up). The child has to be self-reliant in order to please the parent. However, the more self-reliant the child is, the more the parent withdraws, feeling that the child no longer needs so much of their time and attention. (Emotional needs are not recognized as valid reasons to detract the parents from their other duties.) Therefore, being responsible and reliable also brings about the loss of "love," and so the child is in a quandry—whatever he does, he loses.

Saturn has to do with time and with maturity, making especially strong aspects to its original place every seven years—at 7, when we're really getting involved with school, at 14 when we're teenagers, and at 21, when we're legally adults. Naturally, for the Venus-Saturn person, each time

Saturn aspects its natal place, it forms another aspect to natal Venus as well; so each of these periods of growth, accomplishment, maturing, and taking on of responsibility is also marked by a loss of love. Each stage of maturation brings progressively less parental support and love, and the person is left to face each new stage alone. Experiences like this make for a person who basically doesn't trust others to fill any of their needs and who feels there is no way that they can be loved. They learned from their parents that they can't be loved if they aren't Saturnian, and that they can't be loved if they *are* either, so the logical conclusion would be that they can't be loved at all. The person feels deprived of love, and as protection against that painful feeling may build a wall against the world. The wall winds up reinforcing their feeling of being unlovable, because other people sooner or later stop trying to get through it.

The positive side of a Venus-Saturn aspect is that you don't get older, you get better. A late bloomer, you may be a plain, awkward teenager but suddenly become a beauty in your thirties and forties. Nor do you age as harshly as other folks—you'll probably look years younger than your peers. Your popularity improves with age too—seriousness is problematic for an adolescent, but is expected of the middle-aged and older. Through that serious approach to life, you can also achieve a great deal that earns you respect.

Venus and Uranus: The person with this aspect has to learn to "hang loose" in his relationships or suffer a great deal. Plain old sock-darning, rent-paying love doesn't interest them—they want excitement, glitter, and variety. Furthermore there's often an attraction to the slightly dangerous, potentially violent type of person just for the sheer adrenaline rush. They generally relate to people vastly different from themselves, sometimes the kinky, rebellious, nonconformist type who'll jump on a motorcycle and wheelie off into the sunset.

Now this is all great fun as long as you don't get possessive and don't want roots and commitments—but insist on such things with Uranian people, and you'll suddenly find yourself alone. This aspect is marked by sudden changes and disruptions in the love life—no Golden Anniversary celebrations likely. And don't expect the person to be there for you. . . your Uranian partner is too detached to relate to your feelings. So what's in it for you? You're the one who's doing the choosing, and you chose this paragon, out of the itching of that Venus-Uranus aspect. If you want more security, you may have to learn to care for people who aren't quite as stimulating, but who are more likely to be there when you need them.

What psychological factors and what childhood experiences lead to a pattern like this? Uranus might signify a broken home or a parent who came and went unpredictably, no doubt an erratic parent, and perhaps a home where violence and upheaval were present. Often, the violence and upheaval somehow became sexualized, perhaps through some unconscious seductiveness on the part of the erratic parent toward the child. What positives are there in this aspect? It results in quite a cosmopolitan experience and the ability to get along with many different kinds of people. Often you come in contact with interesting and stimulating people who broaden your mind. You can also doubtlessly get along with young people and help them through the turmoil of growing up. And you are open to new acquaintances.

Venus and Neptune: Frequently a savior/martyr complex exists in love relationships under this aspect. You choose people you think you can reform—Neptune/twelfth house types of people like ex-cons, alcoholics, invalids, or severely disturbed people. A pattern of choices like these often leaves you hurt, because your goals of reform or cure are unrealistic. After you're hurt a few times by alcoholics, you may swear off them, but proceed to some other Neptunian type, like ex-cons.

Before you can stop "magically" picking out partner after partner that fits such a pattern, you've got to become aware of your part in the situation and of why you may unconsciously need to pick people who will hurt you. You are not a victim, although with this aspect you secretly enjoy believing you are—you're one of those people who enjoy the role of martyr. (With this aspect your psychic sensitivity is very keen, even if you're using it for self-destructive choices.) Despite all kinds of clues, your neurotic needs cause you to blind yourself to the true nature of these people. Perhaps people like these unconsciously make you feel quite superior and at the same time like a very special, terribly compassionate super-being who will work the miracle of cure.

Often, too, the problem is related to the model of love-relationships you saw at home. As a social worker, I found that almost every woman whose husband was an alcoholic had a father or some other significant person in her childhood who drank heavily. The masochistic pleasure her mother derived from being the rescuer and rock of Gibraltar for the family transmitted itself to the daughter and to her vision of what marriage was like. She wound up selecting either a man who drank too much but "gave it up for me"—gave it up, that is, until the first bloom of love wore off. Or else she chose a man of whom she says, "I didn't know he drank," even though she should have been extremely familiar with the signs and symptoms because of her own father. The wives of drug addicts show similar dynamics. The "way out" for a Venus-Neptune person is to relate compassionately to such troubled people without feeling the necessity to rescue them and play the martyr in such a relationship. A better choice of mate might be someone who personifies the positive traits of Neptune—spirituality, creativity, and dedication.

Venus and Pluto: With this combination, you alternate between extremes—you're either a loner or get into symbiotic relationships so smothering and possessive that it's hard to remain an individual. Jealousy, suspicion, and lack of trust are usually present, along with brooding and bitterness over former lovers you drove away with the smothering routine. "Til death do us part," is your motto in any relationship, so you find it hard to forget—or forgive—the ones that got away. Yet, your very intensity and neediness overwhelm people and make you wind up "Alone again, naturally." Control is also a very important issue in your relationships—if you don't have it, you'll work until you get it. If the other person is in control, you exercise the final word in control—by leaving. Obviously this manner of relating to other people leaves them (and you) without much freedom or individuality, and it's not likely to make you happy. Letting up on your control and possessiveness is hard work, but otherwise it will warp your relationships. (Read the suggestions in the chapter on Pluto).

Summary

Venus has to do with our ability to love and to relate to others. Sharing, cooperation, equality, and harmony all go into a good relationship. Love has many pitfalls, and I more than suspect that Venus isn't the easy, beneficent force it's made out to be. It must be approached in as spiritual a manner as any of the outer planets. Personal love is often doomed to failure, but love that is based on spirituality is on the right path. For a description of what love is and ought to be, I can't improve on the description given in First Corinthians, Chapter 13:

Though I speak with the tongues of men and angels, and have not love, I am become as sounding brass or a tinkling cymbal. And though I have the gift of prophecy and understand all mysteries and all knowledge, and though I have all faith so that I could remove mountains and have not Love, I am nothing. And though I bestow all my goods to feed the poor, and though I give my body to be burned, and have not Love, it profits me nothing.

Love suffers long and is kind; love envies not. Love vaunts not itself, is not puffed up, does not behave unseemly, seeks not her own, is not easily provoked, thinks no evil; rejoices not in iniquity, but rejoices in the truth; bears all things, believes all things, hopes all things, endures all things.

Love never fails, but whether there be prophecies, they shall fail, whether there be tongues, they shall cease, whether there be knowledge, it shall vanish away... And now abides faith, hope and love, these are three; but the greatest of all these is Love.

CHAPTER 6

MARS & HEALTHY SELF-ASSERTION

Traditional astrologers have called Mars a "malefic" or evil planet, but I disagree with them on two counts.* First, the division of planets into malefics and benefics is wrong—any planet properly used has its constructive function in our lives and any planet improperly used can be destructive. Second, Mars by itself is neither positive nor negative its key meaning is "directed energy," and the ways we direct it and the targets we choose to direct it toward determine whether it is constructive or destructive. This depends on the basic character of the individual, which requires an understanding of the entire chart, not just Mars and its aspects. Among other things, Mars has to do with anger, competition, and sexuality, and perhaps this is another reason it was designated a malefic. Our culture has yet to become comfortable with these basic urges. In this chapter, we will explore the positive uses of Mars, see where the negative sides of it arise, and consider whether the more difficult manifestations, such as anger, are not also normal and even healthy expressions of human nature. In trying to understand Mars, we will note what some of the theories of modern psychology have to say about anger, aggression and self-assertiveness.

The Symbol for Mars—♂

In trying to understand astrological symbols, I like to get away from stilted phrases like "the circle of spirit" and the "cross of matter." There are very deep meanings in these symbols, but I think they speak more to our subconscious than to our conscious minds if we will open up and let them. I teach beginning astrology to patients at a ghetto treatment center for alcoholics, and, without telling them anything at all about Mars, I had them draw the symbol very large several times. Their observations were quite profound. One said it was perpetual motion outwardly directed; others said it was energetic, forceful, and aggressive. You may want to try this yourself and see the reaction.

---

*Part of this material was originally published as "Mars and Healthy Aggression," *Aquarian Astrology*, Summer 1973 issue, p. 84. Reprinted by permission of CBS Publications, Consumer Publishing Division of CBS, Inc.

It is characteristic of our culture that ♂ has been accepted as the symbol for male. Certainly, if you distort the symbol slightly you get ♂ , which could be a representation of the erect male genitals. A male with an erection is driven by desire, and Mars represents the desires that drive us on. If Mars is accepted as male, though, then what does that say about our culture's view of women? Every woman alive has Mars in her chart and has the same need men do to achieve, compete, and conquer. A woman with a strong Mars, though, is considered too aggressive and masculine. It is only our culture that places this judgement on her, just as it harshly judges men with a strong Venus as too feminine. It is important for people like this to know that it is our culture's hang-up and not their own. It is important, too, for all women to know that it is *human* to get angry, to compete, to have strong sexual needs and to show other traits of Mars, and that it is just our culture which labels these needs "unfeminine."

Mars & Energy

We said earlier that the keywords for Mars are "directed energy." Studying Mars in the chart can show you a great deal about your energy pattern and how to get the most out of it. You can learn to work with it rather than against it. Is it erratic, a la Mars in Aquarius, or slow and steady like Mars in Taurus? The person with Mars in Taurus shouldn't expect to work in spurts or leave things until the last minute . . . they need warm-up time and can't be pushed, so they need to start well in advance. A Mars in Gemini person might need to have more than one thing going in order to stave off boredom, but should recognize that too many things going at once or too much talking can distract them from getting anything done at all. Or, they can accommodate themselves so that boring tasks like ironing can be done while talking on the phone. . . they are perfectly capable of concentrating on two things at once. By analysing and understanding your Mars and its meaning, you can make more effective use of your time and energy.

Watching transits by Mars or transits to your Mars can help you channel those bursts of energy and make the best use of them. I am writing this on a transit of Mars in Virgo squaring my Mercury in Gemini. I made the conscious decision to put that energy to work in writing about Mars. I could have wasted it by getting hung up in housework, fussing and complaining irritably all day, picking a fight, or running up the phone bill by chatting all day. I was tempted by each of those, but said no to them. You can direct your energy, rather than let it direct you, by picking the most positive and constructive use of that Mars transit and saying no to the rest.

Mars & Sexuality

Mars is equated with sexuality in many books on Astrology. I see it as only one type or part of sexuality—the conquest and the penetration. It is the active principle of sex, where you are doing it *to* the other person, with or without their participation. Sex has many other facets—the Venus principles of attraction and sharing, the Moon principle of responding, the Mercury principles of communication and playfulness. . . all things that go into making sex more enjoyable than the Slam-Bam-Thank-You-Mam way that Mars would operate by itself. It would seem that each planet has its own part to play in a fully developed human sexuality. Again, Mars is not only a male prerogative—women can also enjoy taking the initiative sexually and being the more active partner. For both men and women, a study of Mars in your chart can help you discover the kinds of sexual activities that would be most fulfilling. (In fact, undertaking such an analysis is in itself a positive use of Martian initiative.) For example, if you have Mars in Cancer or a Moon-Mars aspect, giving and receiving oral sex may be very pleasurable. Having Mars in Leo might signify that a playful approach or play-acting little sexual dramas would be pleasurable. With Mars in Gemini, talking during sex or in preparation for it would heighten pleasure. By discarding some of the heavy moralistic ideas we've been taught about sex and seriously studying the Mars placement in your chart, you can identify your true sexual needs and find greater sexual fulfillment.

The Constructive Function of Mars

Some of the constructive functions of our lives that Mars represents are action, initiative, leadership, the need to build and accomplish, and the effort toward self-mastery. These are all upward and outward thrusts of energy, like the arrow on the Mars symbol. A person with a strong positive Mars will be energetic, productive, independent, forceful, and creative. When Mars is functioning in these helpful ways, I would consider it a benefic. How could we accomplish anything without it?

People with Mars or Aries strong in their chart are often very active. This can be wonderful and lead to accomplishing a great deal if the energy is directed and disciplined. Many of these people, however, are in love with action for its own sake. They do things just to be doing something, without thinking it through. As a result, they don't accomplish much that is worthwhile and their efforts are wasted. Sometimes their needless activity even detracts from getting to work on goals that are meaningful to them. Unless your efforts are centered, you may be busy all the time and yet not accomplish anything. Mars is exalted in Capricorn, and the lesson this teaches us is that we get the most out of our energy and activity when they are disciplined and planned out ahead.

Leadership is another trait attributed to Aries and other people with a strong Mars. Aries people want to be number one in all things, and their pioneering spirit makes them take the lead. I owe to Rod Chase the insight that in order to be a good leader, paradoxically, you need to be a good follower. He notes that orchestra leaders follow the musical score, actors follow the script, military leaders follow the orders of those above them, and spiritual leaders are obedient to God. Actually, many famous generals (e.g., Eisenhower) have been Libra rather than Aries. Mars would charge rashly into battle when sometimes it is better to wait or even beat a strategic retreat. All things are good in balance—the positive side of Mars in a leader is courage, vitality and keenness.

If you feel that someone has difficulties with some of the areas mentioned above, perhaps a detailed analysis of Mars in that person's chart would help uncover the reasons why. Maybe the person hasn't yet begun to express the positive side of his Mars. *Re*directing energy into more positive channels can heal many of the problems people experience with their Mars. As an example, let's take Mars in Pisces or a Mars-Neptune aspect. Individuals using it negatively might be spending most of their energy in the pursuit of drugs or alcohol, to the detriment of the rest of their development. The more positive expression might be such things as creative work on art, music, or dance, helping disturbed or ill people, or in following the spiritual path. Mars in Pisces or Mars-Neptune people are often lethargic and aimless, but once they aim for positive Neptunian goals like the ones above, they can have a tremendous spiritual vitality, and their lives take on direction and meaning that were previously lacking.

Another example might be Mars in Scorpio in the third, a combination I've heard described as "a black belt in tongue karate." Negative uses might be sarcasm, feuding with relatives, or digging up gossip about the neighbors—all bringing misery to the person who has it because they invite disputes and other negative vibrations into the environment. A more positive channel for this energy might be studying, writing, or teaching about psychology or the occult. It would also be good for research, or even writing mystery stories. If the person's energies were channeled into fascinating activities like these, there would be little time or enthusiasm left for disputes.

A third example would be Mars in Aquarius in the sixth. Before this is properly directed, the person might have an erratic work history, be unable to conform to rules, and have explosive arguments with the boss that lead to being fired. How can this be used constructively? Correct vocational choice is essential. It can't be a traditional, routine setting, but one that offers a great deal of freedom, flexibility, variety, and mental stimulation. The person needs to be on his own, rather than heavily supervised, perhaps in a free lance situation. A modern, technical field such as computers might be indicated. The person might even be an astrologer. If these conditions are met, this could be an outstanding worker—Mars in the sixth can be energy and initiative poured into the job, and Aquarius shows creativity and innovation.

When you see Mars in a difficult placement or aspect in a chart, don't let the negative interpretations in books discourage you. Mars has its positive expression for each sign, house, and aspect, and you can uncover them if you think about it. Work toward the positive expression and you'll be much less troubled by the negative side. Old habits die hard, and we take a step backward now and then, but at least the thrust of your life will be upward, and you'll be drawing positive experiences toward you instead of negative.

Mars & Aggression

When the outward thrust of Mars is carried to an extreme, it can be headstrong, rash, careless, and pugnacious. The directness and sharpness of its thrust can be carried to the point of sarcasm and even cruelty. These are more aggressive and even hostile expressions of what is essentially a neutral energy. Psychologists have studied aggression intensively in recent years, and looking at their findings may give us insight into how Mars functions and how its energies get diverted into more negative forms. One well-known theory is that aggression is a learned behavior and that the key factor in producing aggression is frustration, especially of basic needs or drives.

We can observe this in a small child trying unsuccessfully to get his mother's attention. He may first speak to her, then touch her, then tug at her with increasing intensity, and finally, when none of this succeeds, bite or kick her out of frustration and rage. The initial intent was not a hostile one, but the severe frustration drove him to a hostile act. The same principle can be observed in the aggressive behavior of adults, whether overt or extremely subtle in expression. Consider, for example, the irate verbalizations of a frustrated driver caught in a traffic jam when in a hurry to get somewhere. Aggressive patterns learned in childhood can carry over into adult life and be acted on long after the original frustrations are forgotten.

How does this theory—that frustration leads to aggression—relate to the planet Mars? Mars is the basic outward thrust of the personality—the energy and desire that is directed toward some goal. When we are blocked or frustrated in reaching that goal, as we must often be in the real world, the angry and aggressive side of Mars results. Thus, we can see that Mars per se is not anger, but anger is a secondary expression of Mars energy when it is not allowed to proceed directly toward its goal. Anger and aggression are normal, inevitable emotions and not the taboo things our society has made them. They are facts of life resulting from the reality that we cannot always have what we want or do what we want to do—nor would it necessarily be desirable if we could. In this culture, however, anger is considered dangerous, shameful, and uncivilized, an emotion we must hide at all costs from each other and very frequently even from ourselves.

If we know which sign of the zodiac Mars occupies in an individual's chart, we can get some idea of how the person has learned to deal with anger—easily and openly, as for instance with a well-aspected Mars in Aries; diffusely and self-destructively, as with a poorly-aspected Mars in Pisces; or to suppress it at all costs while it ferments underground, as with a Mars in Scorpio in the twelfth. These are all placements that we can learn to use positively, but work may be needed to divert the energy from negative uses.

The consequences of suppressing most of our anger can be destructive to our mental and physical health. In his very readable paperback, *The Angry Book*, psychiatrist Theodore Isaac Rubin talks about the many ways we hide anger from ourselves and the distorted ways it is then expressed, from neuroses to psychosomatic illnesses, from addictions to psychoses. Rubin is saying that suppressed or unconscious anger doesn't go away but accumulates and can erupt in destructive ways. These ideas reveal a great deal about the more destructive or malefic characteristics attributed to Mars. If someone is carrying around a big load of anger all the time, something drastic is likely to happen when Mars makes an aspect to his chart by transit or when he meets someone whose Mars makes contact with one of his planets. The added force of Mars, not necessarily destructive in itself, can be the spark that sets off the suppressed rage. The fury that follows is attributed to Mars, when actually it is due to the unhealthy accumulation of anger.

The person who is able to be aware of, express, and regulate his anger in a healthy way never builds up to such a massive explosion, so a transit from Mars does not affect him so destructively. He is also freer to show more of the positive characteristics of Mars described earlier, because the suppression of Mars in one area freezes, poisons, or clamps down on the other Mars functions. Again and again in his practice, Rubin has seen how patients who learn to deal with their suppressed anger become more energetic, more productive, and more fully expressed sexually. Their neurotic symptoms disappear and they begin to live fuller lives (i.e., they begin to use their Mars in positive ways).

I realize, of course, that it is much easier to tell someone they must learn to deal with their anger than it is to do it. In some cases, psychotherapy, encounter groups, or some other kind of outside intervention may be needed. It can be helpful to read some of the current books on aggression (e.g., *Creative Aggression*) or on how to fight (e.g., *The Intimate Enemy*). Nor am I giving you carte blanche to vent your hostility on everything in sight, as that can be just as destructive as always suppressing your anger. Where astrology can help, however, is in identifying the problems the person has with anger and uncovering the causes. Suppose a person has Mars conjunct Neptune, where Neptune rules the tenth. This could be someone who had an irrational and possibly even psychotic authority figure to deal with in the home, and who as a result fears they will go crazy if they lose their temper. Another example might be someone with Mars conjunct Pluto in Leo in the first, with Pluto ruling the fourth. In this case, a parent, possibly the mother, actively suppressed the child's aggressive and angry behavior, so that the person unconsciously fears there will be heavy retribution for any anger they show. At worst, they may even fear that anger will lead to murder—either their own, or the person they get angry at. As we learn from Rubin's book, however, it is not *anger* that leads to drastic consequences such as these but its *suppression* and accumulation.

Mars & Irritability

I see irritability as a rather distorted form of anger. The irritable person finds constant sources of annoyance in the daily environment, but I think the cause is an underlying anger that has been there for a long time, perhaps since early childhood. Deciphering the sign, house placement, and aspects of Mars in the chart may help unravel the wellspring of irritability so that it can be worked on more directly. There are some signs where Mars is less irritable than others—Mars in Taurus or Leo, for instance, aren't very irritable unless they form difficult aspects, such as to Uranus or Saturn.

One way of finding the underlying cause for irritability is via the concepts of Albert Ellis, a psychotherapist who developed his own style of treatment called Rational Emotive Therapy. He talks about the irrational "sentences" we carry around in our unconscious that cause us to behave neurotically. The person with Mars in Cancer, for instance, might be going around fuming because they believe, "I've got to take care of everybody and nobody will take care of me!" This sentence is irrational on two counts. First of all, whoever told you that you have to be Supermother and take care of everyone around you? There's no law that says that you do, and in a lot of cases, they'd survive very well without your help. Second, if nobody ever takes care of you, you are making neurotic choices in friends and partners and unconsciously selecting people who only take and can't give.

The Mars in Virgo person's sentence may go like this, "Things are all wrong here, and *I've* always got to be the one to set them right!" This is a fallacious belief for two reasons. First, who says they are all wrong? You? Who made you the judge of what is right for other people? What feels wrong or uncomfortable for you may be the most effective way for someone else to operate or may be the source of their particular genius. (Do you know that the floor of Abraham Lincoln's law office was so dirty that seeds dropped there would sprout?) Second, who or what says you have to be the one to set things right? If it is truly wrong and dysfunctional, rather than just not perfect by your standards, then it will feel wrong to the people involved too and they can be motivated to work with you. That is the only real avenue to change, not forcing your way upon others. Isn't it a kind of ego trip to feel that you are the one and only person who really can straighten things out?

Mars in the other signs may be carrying irrational sentences around too, that you can discover when you are looking for the source of irritability. Mars in Capricorn might be saying, "Doesn't anyone else ever think ahead?" Mars in Aquarius might be asking, "Why is everyone always telling me what to do?" The concept of uncovering the irrational sentence is discussed in the many books by Albert Ellis, and I would recommend them, as these concepts can be applied to many other areas of the chart besides Mars.

Mars & Self-Assertion

There are many books out on the subject of self-assertion (*Don't Say Yes When You Mean No, The Self-Assertive Woman*, etc.) and there are even groups you can go to which will teach you to be self-assertive. This strikes me as the most balanced and healthy expression of Mars. It is clearly related to Mars, in that the contrasts are always made between self-assertion, aggression, and hostility. *Self-assertive* persons know how to stand up for their own rights and desires without attacking other people or running over them. If they do not wish to do something, they say no rather than agree and be angry the whole time they are doing it. If someone is doing something to them that makes them angry, they tell them (again not in an attacking but a factual way) rather than suppress the anger until it builds up to something major.

People with Mars or Aries strong in their charts are self-assertive by nature, unless there are severe restrictions or difficulties with it (e.g., Sun in Aries opposite Neptune or Mars in the first conjunct Saturn). Other people, such as those with Mars in Pisces or Mars in the twelfth, can have serious difficulty in asserting themselves and do so only in twisted ways. The passive-aggressive person might be one example—the type who expresses aggression or anger through dragging their heels, "forgetting" to do things, or failing. (Even a psychotic episode or a drunken binge can be an indirect way of asserting yourself—"I will no longer live by your rules.") These are very distorted and self-destructive ways of standing up for your right to do things your own way. How much better to learn to say no in the first place. For those with a difficult Mars, help may be needed to accomplish this.

Making Peace with "The God of War"

We have tried to understand why Mars' more outwardly negative sides develop and how we can work out of them. The more positive and constructive functions of Mars have been shown to be essential to the whole, healthy person. Some parts of Mars—like anger, competition, and sexual drive—may still be uncomfortable to many in our culture, but they are as normal and natural as breathing and just about as inevitable. To label them bad and try to suppress them is just as damaging as deciding that you despise one of your kidneys and having it taken out. Mars is neither a malefic nor a benefic, it just *is*.

CHAPTER 7

JUPITER — THE OVERRATED BENEFIC

We're going to find out that Jupiter often means OVER-doing things—OVEReating, OVERdrinking, and generally OVERindulging. Jupiter itself in astrology is often OVER-done—we OVERrate its helpfulness and OVERestimate how much it's going to do for us when it transits our charts. We will even find out in this chapter that Saturn has as much to do with good luck and success as Jupiter does. . . and that Jupiter, believe it or not, can create its own kind of bad luck. Through our explorations of Jupiter, we'll be aiming (like the Sagittarian archer) for a more balanced view of this planet, which is neither malefic nor benefic, but a little bit of both.

In astrology, Jupiter is the planet of growth and expansion, and Jupiter people can be quite large. In the solar system, Jupiter is the giant. It is 1300 times the size of the earth; all the other planets in the solar system could fit inside it. There is some indication (Velikovsky's theories) that Jupiter is not like the other planets but could be star material. One confirmation of this is the fact that it gives off nine times the radiation it receives from the Sun. (In astrology, Jupiter is associated with benevolence, and spiritual teachers tell us that we get back ninefold or tenfold what we give.)

Jupiter & the Liver

In medical astrology, Jupiter rules the liver, and there is much to be said of this relationship. Just as Jupiter is the largest planet in the solar system, the liver is the largest organ in the body. The liver has a great many functions: 1) it helps us digest and absorb our food by secreting bile, 2) it stores and distributes excess nourishment, 3) it filters out toxic material, and 4) helps us form and break down blood. The planet Jupiter also performs vital functions in our lives, some of which are similar to the liver. It is wisdom gained from digesting and absorbing experiences, so that we grow from our mistakes. It is also the wisdom not to repeat damaging (toxic) mistakes.

Jupiter is exalted in Cancer, the sign that rules nourishment. Jupiter rules wisdom, and the liver knows when the body has had too much nourishment and either stores or destroys the excess. A well-regulated liver knows how much is too much—and so does a well-aspected Jupiter; but both a diseased liver and an off-balance Jupiter cope poorly with excess and can no longer regulate it properly. Jupiter is concerned with growth and expansion; when we eat and drink to excess, the liver expands also to compensate. After years of overindulgence, the liver enlarges permanently and gets sick. If we "live it up" too long, we get liverish. Jupiter people often don't know when to stop, and many of them wind up with liver trouble.

Jupiter — the Broad View

Sagittarians love to roam and also seem scattered all over the place in their thoughts and speech—but if you are able to pin them down, there is a connection. Jupiter's meanings also seem scattered and far-reaching, but we'll find the connections as we go along. For instance, we'll discover in a later section how good luck—one of the supposed attributes of Jupiter—has as its component parts some of the other meanings of Jupiter, like enthusiasm, wisdom, philosophy, and benevolence. Another apparently unconnected set of meanings of Jupiter and the ninth house, which is associated with it, is higher education, foreign travel, law and religion. In the medieval era, this hodgepodge would never even have been questioned, it would be so obvious. If we take a historical perspective (as Jupiterians love to do), we can see how these diverse concepts are clearly connected.

During the medieval era and before, centers of learning were few and far between, and people had to travel long distances to get an education. Even now, we say that travel broadens, recognizing that exposure to other cultures and other ways of doing things gives us a broader perspective on life and on the standards and values of our own culture. The connection between religion and travel has always been felt by those who made pilgrimages. Many important religions travelled far from their place of origin and were brought to the new locale by foreign travellers or missionaries. The connection between religion and education has loosened in only the past forty years. In medieval times, the only educated people were monks and nobles, and the monks taught the nobles. Many young men who wanted an education would join a monastery to get it. The first colleges, even in this country, were founded by the church.

The connections between religion and law have also been obscured by time, but are quite important. The first laws were based on religious edicts, like the Mosaic code. The founders of our country made a specific issue of the separation of church and state, in order to form a truly independent government. Even now, the church has a powerful legislative lobby, such as in the anti-abortion battles going on here and in the anti-divorce law that was only recently repealed in Catholic Italy. Law and foreign countries are connected in that certain codes of law, such as the Napoleonic code, were adopted or influential in forming the laws of many foreign lands. Law and education are connected in that law was one of the earliest and foremost courses of study in the European universities.

There are even, you will be surprised to learn, connections between education, foreign places, religion, and that other Jupiterian pursuit, gambling. These interesting insights into the place gambling played in founding our nation are cited by Mario Puzo in *Inside Las Vegas:*[1]

> The sailing of the Mayflower to colonize the new world was financed by a lottery in England. Yale, Harvard, and Dartmouth were built with funds raised by a lottery. Lotteries supplied funds to pay the Revolutionary army and win our Independence.

1. Mario Puzo, *Inside Las Vegas*, Grosset and Dunlap, 1976. This quote and others in this chapter are taken from the excerpt in *Book Digest* May '77, pp. 33-57.

Even today, of course, some of the proceeds of legalized lotteries go to finance education. In other states, Bingo and "Las Vegas Nights" are legal only so long as they are run by a church. Finally, churches and other charities are perpetually selling chances on some long-shot dream car they are raffling off.

In the previous paragraphs, we have seen how the various meanings of Jupiter (higher education, foreign travel, law, religion, and gambling) have been related to one another historically, through the concrete ties and dealings each has had with the other. On a less concrete level, however, these diverse realms of Jupiter are also related. They all arise out of the human being's urge to go beyond the ego world and relate to the larger context of society. With Jupiter, issues are no longer just of self (the Sun and Moon) or of self and other (Mercury, Venus, Mars), but of self within the context of all humanity and within the global view of life. Jupiter in the various signs can show how we seek to expand and grow within society. For instance, I know of an English professor who has Jupiter in Gemini. A Jupiter in Pisces person might grow a great deal by serving people in prisons or other institutions. A Jupiter in Capricorn person can serve a vital societal function as an administrator.

Jupiter & Gambling

Jupiter people love to gamble, and some, especially those with Mars-Jupiter aspects, can be compulsive about it. In moderation, though, gambling can even have some positive effects, which we'll see in a moment. Jupiter is correlated with optimism, and pessimistic people rarely do much gambling. The cockeyed optimist keeps on playing, despite repeated losses, even knowing the odds are against him, because he basically doesn't believe he can lose. Maybe he just lost a bundle, but this time, mind you, he's sure to win. And don't tell him any different, because he'll turn a deaf ear. "Trying to jinx me or something?" Closely related to optimism is hope, and none of us could go on without it. For many people stuck in slums, in boring jobs, or in life situations where they feel hopeless, a little gambling keeps them alive. That quarter a ghetto dweller puts on a number gives him an "up," a reason to live through today, and a hope that tomorrow will magically put an end to the nightmare he lives in.

Mario Puzo (who wrote *The Godfather*) was once a compulsive gambler and writes about it eloquently and with a great deal of insight. In his book, *Inside Las Vegas*, he says:

> What possesses a group of mature people who know what life is all about to think that gambling can solve their problems? Desperation, that's what, and something to put a little spice in your life.
>
> [In psychiatric explanations for gambling] . . . what gets left out are the solace and pleasure it's brought countless millions living in worlds without hope and without those dreams essential to life.

People who have more to live for, who have hope for the future, are not so prone to compulsive gambling. Puzo confirms this, in explaining why he quit gambling:

> Now for the first time in my life, making more money than I have ever made in my life . . . I have come to the decision that I cannot afford, economically, to gamble. The simple reason being that to gamble is to risk, that is to approach the "ruin factor." When I was poor the ruin factor was not important. Hell, I was ruined anyway.

Closely akin to this connection between poverty and gambling is the fixation low income people have on that other Jupiterian long shot, the lawsuit. For many, the only way they can envision out of poverty is to hit the lottery or win a big lawsuit. In a similar way, many people from poor countries throughout the world have acted upon the Jupiterian hope of going to a foreign country to seek their fortune.

As we've seen, Jupiter is related to faith and religion. The connection gambling has with faith is easy to see—faith is an upwardly directed extension of hope and optimism. But religion? Here are some very interesting insights by Mario Puzo:

The truth is that gambling is a primitive religious instinct peculiar to our species . . . Religious leaders, those supreme hustlers of the long shot, are revered, but gamblers are sneered at because most people think of gambling as a foolish vice.

It's not that you want to lose what you've won, it's just that you don't believe it's possible to lose. When winning you are convinced God loves you. It is as close as I have ever come in my life to a religious feeling. Or to being a wonder-struck child.

Is that so different from these religious fanatics who think that after death they will go to their particular heaven?

I think the whole magic power of gambling lies in its essential purity of endeavor, in its absence of guilt. No matter what our character, no matter what our behavior, no matter if we are ugly, unkind, murderers, saints, guilty sinner, foolish or wise, we *can* get lucky.

Ready to accept that religion and gambling are connected? After all, many of the tools of divination we use in spiritual studies are ruled by the laws of chance—laying out the Tarot cards, throwing the *I Ching*, or setting up a horary chart. Yet we believe that some power is arranging the cards, the coins, or the horary chart into a spiritually meaningful pattern that will elucidate our lives. Is that so far removed from the faith a gambler exercises?

To gamble successfully, you have to have another Jupiter trait—wisdom. You have to know the odds; in the numbers game, for instance, your chances of winning are 1 in 999, but in blackjack you have a better than even chance. You have to know that your chances of winning at the lotteries and slot machines are miniscule. If you still enjoy the thrill of it, that rush of adrenaline while you wait for the results, do it as long as you can regard it as entertainment. But the compulsive gambler will believe he can beat the odds and will pour large sums of money into such hopeless games. The bad luck that can come from gambling, then, also relates to Jupiterian traits—overindulgence, overconfidence, and foolish optimism. In its place and in moderation, gambling can have some positive effects. It gives hope to the hopeless, excitement to people whose lives are dull, and a feeling of divine grace in those moments when we actually win. As we saw earlier, gambling has even financed some worthwhile institutions. As with all things, however, balance and wisdom are needed to keep what can be a harmless pastime from becoming self-destructive.

Jupiter & Saturn — Co-rulers of Luck & Success

I've been a fairly lucky person all my life, and once, after a run of especially good luck, I set about analysing it.[2] I felt that by understanding my luck, I could not only increase it for myself, but also teach my heretofore unconscious "methods" to others who haven't been so fortunate. Naturally, I thought a great deal about Jupiter, the planet traditionally associated with good luck, but I was quite surprised to discover Saturn has as much or more to do with luck as Jupiter. Saturn? I know it's "the greater malefic" and "the grim reaper," and it's supposed to bring on all kinds of misfortune. If you really get into it, though, Saturn doesn't bring anything on you that you haven't already brought on yourself . . . and if what you've done is lay the *foundations* for good luck, then Saturn will bring you better and longer lasting "luck" than you ever had under Jupiter.

Let me give you an example. Saturn once was square my midheaven for six weeks from the twelfth house. Many astrologers would say I was in for some real *bad* luck from the "old taskmaster" there. What happened was perhaps the luckiest break in my life so far—I got promoted to head social worker in the hospital where I worked. I happened to be the only person on the scene with *most* of the right qualifications when the position became vacant—and I had been working there only four months at the time! In the normal course of events, I wouldn't have been eligible for that kind of position for about five more years. Obviously I also have the ability, or they would have gone outside to hire someone rather than give me the opportunity to try,

---

2. This segment originally appeared in *Astrology Guide*, 8/75 issue, as "Change Your Luck—Now & Forever." It is reprinted with the permission of Sterling Publications, Inc. © 1975 Sterling Publications.

but it was luck that I was the person who just happened to be there. So Saturn isn't necessarily the bad influence people think it is.

Actually, a lot of what other people label "luck" isn't Jupiter at all, but very Saturnian in nature... not pure luck, but hard work, self-discipline, and preparation that finally paid off. You may have sat up nights polishing your writing technique. Then when you are finally good enough to break into the important magazines, the grasshoppers say, "I wish I had your luck!" It reminds me of the statement I heard once by Bill Macey, the T.V. husband of Maude. He said, "I put in 25 years of hard work to become an overnight success." Isn't Saturn as much responsible for that kind of "luck" as Jupiter?

Another Saturnian characteristic that contributes a great deal to "luck" is *timing*. You may have everything going for you—a great idea, good financial backing, all the right people working on it—but unless the timing is right, you may fail. There is a saying that goes, "There is nothing so powerful as an idea whose time has come." This is as true in your career or personal life as in anything else. The "lucky" person knows instinctively the right time to ask for a raise, to launch that campaign, or to make that long-contemplated move. Life can be like a game of Slapjack—unless you have that splitsecond timing, you can miss out on many great opportunities. Other Saturnian traits are also important, like persistence and follow-through. You may have the nicest stroke of luck come your way, but miss out unless you are already prepared to take advantage of it; or you may actually be given the opportunity, but unless you have the self-discipline to follow up with some hard work, the luck will evaporate.

In fact, what I've really come to understand is that Saturn and Jupiter are the co-rulers of luck, and they are intricately related. This is quite clear if you go back to the actual symbols for the two planets. The original symbol for Jupiter is made up of the crescent of receptivity $\supset$ and the cross of matter $+$ combined as follows: $\text{2}\!\!\!\downarrow$. The original symbol for Saturn is made of the same two elements, the crescent of receptivity and the cross of matter, this written $\hbar$ or $\hbar$. When written $\hbar$, its relationship to Jupiter is even more obvious, as they are inverted versions of each other. Some of the implications of this interrelationship will become clearer as we go along.

Let's spend some time now looking at the component meanings of the planet Jupiter to see how it will increase our understanding of luck. One of the meanings of Jupiter is wisdom, and I have a strong feeling that a great deal of what other people label "luck" is actually wisdom, foresight, intelligence or plain good sense. No one wants to admit that they weren't as smart as you were about something, so they say, "You were lucky." I suspect that the person who is "lucky" with stocks or real estate, for example, is often the person with the foresight to see what investments will pay off. Wisdom and foresight are also involved in another attribute of the lucky person. I always say that luck is being the right person in the right place at the right time. . . but some kind of canny evaluation had gone on there for the "lucky" person to have known, consciously or unconsciously, that he was the right person, that this was the right place, and to have been there at the psychologically right time. Doubtlessly, I have also been the wrong person in the wrong place at the wrong time, but I have never suffered any real "bad luck" from it, because I have the sense not to compound the error by investing much of myself in it or staying very long.

This brings me to another component of good luck—not one you find in the lists of attributes of Jupiter, but if you go back to the basic symbol for Jupiter, you will wonder why it has been ignored for so long. Receptivity—the crescent of receptivity—is the first thing you draw in making the symbol for Jupiter, and I have come to realize that receptivity is a large part of my good luck. If you have a closed mind and insist that things can only be done one way, you are limiting yourself and you are limiting your opportunities. You might be the right person in the right place at the right time, but if you sit there and refuse to even consider the right idea, you will lose out, and the more receptive person will grab up the "luck" and run with it.

One part of receptivity is the ability to flow with things. It's not wishywashiness I'm talking about... I'm out there working hard and I have some general, long-range goals in mind, but my specific goals for today are up for change at any time in the light of new information or experience. A lot of my "lucky breaks" came about because I am willing to change or postpone my game plan at the drop of a hat if something better comes along, whereas others may spend a lot of time dithering about it and lose the chance. People who aren't lucky are often the opposite of receptive—having traits something like "friction" or "resistance" in physics. These people can't flow with life because they put so many things in the way—old ideas and patterns of behavior prefaced by "I can't"/"I won't"/"I should"/"I shouldn't"/"We've always"/"We've never" and so on and on and on. All these preconceived notions about how to do things get in the way, because luck often depends on your receptivity to a new idea. I am not saying you should sacrifice moral principle; rather, I'm saying you should sacrifice outworn and outmoded ideas about yourself, about ways to do things and about courses of action. Don't be bound to something just because you've always done it that way.

As we've seen, gambling is attributed to Jupiter, and you have to be willing to gamble on something in order to have any luck at all—good or bad. We're not just talking about cards and dice, of course, we're talking about all the risks you take in your personal life. If you don't dare to risk yourself, you'll never move ahead. Jupiter by itself only shows our urge to gamble—and many people gamble when they shouldn't—but this is where Saturn again plays its part in good luck. The positive Saturnian instinctively takes only the calculated risk, betting generally on the sure thing that is most likely to pay off. This part of the reason the professional gambler is consistently "lucky," and I think all successful people are professional gamblers at heart.

Openness and gregariousness are also Jupiter traits, and they play a part in success too. One executive[3] has analyzed the circumstances that led to the big job offers in successful executives' lives. He found that, in the majority of cases, they arose through a chain of acquaintances. He found that lucky people were gregarious and took an interest in people. In turn, their openness also made it easy for other people to approach them in a friendly manner. He concludes:

> The bigger your web of friendly connections, the greater your odds of finding some pot-of-gold opportunity. Actor Kirk Douglas, for example, got his first big break through an earlier contact with a then-unknown actress, Lauren Bacall. She was only one of the people whom the gregarious young Douglas had befriended. But by befriending many people, he increased the chances that a helpful Bacall would turn up!

Apparently, then, that old saying about "It's who you know that counts," is true, but you make your own luck by making positive connections with people—not that this should be our purpose in making friends or being helpful, but it can be an outgrowth of it.

Optimism and enthusiasm are also associated with Jupiter, and their relationship to good luck is very significant. Enthusiasm is contagious and makes others more receptive to you and your ideas. Out of two equally qualified people, who is more likely to be hired, the depressed, apathetic person or the enthusiastic ball of fire? Thus, enthusiastic persons often have more "luck" coming their way—they land the job, they make the sale, they meet their loves.

What does optimism have to do with luck? It's considered quite fashionable these days to be a pessimist, to be down on any new idea before it's even tried, and to be skeptical about everything. The people who think this way

---

3. Max Gunther, "Five Ways to Improve Your Luck," *Readers Digest*, May 1977, pp. 77-80.

constantly squelch their own best ideas and impulses and never take any of the risks you have to take to be lucky. If you want to do that to yourself, that's your privilege, but what concerns me is that the "fashionable" people constantly do it to other people and wind up discouraging the creativity this world really needs.

Yes, optimism does contribute to good luck. The luck people have had with things like positive thinking, the chant *nam myoho renge kyo* and the authentic lucky talisman are all based on the deep occult principle that your outer experience is shaped by your "thought forms" . . . your persistent patterns of thinking. If you "hold the thought" that you are going to be lucky, your chances of good luck are increased. If the thought you are holding is "I have nothing but bad luck," that will prove out too, and bad luck will follow you around like the black cloud that always followed that character in Li'l Abner.

This leads us naturally into another area that Jupiter rules—philosophy. What does being philosophical have to do with luck? Well, our experience only has relevance in terms of how we evaluate it. If you believe that you are a lucky person, you evaluate your experiences as "lucky" more often than the pessimistic person, even when the experiences are not basically very different. I, for instance, happen to consider myself very lucky that some of the things I passionately desired years ago never came to pass. In the light of greater experience and insight, I can see now that they would have been devastating. A pessimistic person, suffering exactly the same disappointment, might never see that it would have been bad for him if he'd gotten it and might go through the rest of his life brooding about this as just another example of "my rotten luck." I am philosophical enough, then, to see that my long-range good fortune has little to do with the subjective emotions and disappointments of the moment that pessimists cling to as proof of their bad luck. What effect would this philosophical approach or the lack of it have on current or future "luck?" Insofar as it affects our self-concept and our willingness to take risks, the belief that you are basically lucky or unlucky often becomes a self-fulfilling prophecy.

Along with philosophy, benevolence is often pointed to as a characteristic of Jupiter. Many of the great financiers, like the original Rockefeller, built their vast fortunes on the principle of tithing—right from the beginning when they, like you, "didn't have it to give." They didn't wait until they had money to start giving, and neither should you. "Give if you want to receive," is the clear message of Bible verses like Luke 7:38: "Give and it shall be given unto you; good measure, pressed down, shaken together, and running over. For with the same measure that ye mete it shall be measured to you again." Isn't it true in many things—the more you put into something the more you get out of it? The benefits of giving are too complex to be covered fully here. Saturn again has its part in helping you give responsibly rather than indiscriminately. Indiscriminate giving often has a bad effect—both on the giver and the receiver.

There is another kind of luck I frequently have that must be a combination of Jupiter and Saturn. One of my mottos is, "Virtue is its own reward," because I often have a stroke of luck when I am doing something disagreeable and tedious, often for someone else. For instance, in attempting to give a responsible answer, complete with statistics, to a reader who disagreed vehemently with something I wrote, I came up with enough material and ideas for another good article. If I had ignored or angrily destroyed the insulting letter, none of my thinking on the matter would have been clarified. I think "virtue" must be at least subconsciously connected with luck in many people's minds, because a frequent comment about a lucky break is, "You must be living right."

Jupiter & Bad Luck

We make our own bad luck just as often and just as surely as we make our good luck. In fact, I know a number of people who go to what looks like a great deal of trouble to do so. One of the ways we do this is by blinding ourselves to the consequences of our actions. We all know people who constantly go around "asking for trouble" and who eventually get it, in spades. This might be seen as negative Jupiter—"pushing your luck" and a kind of stupid optimism or over-confidence, that says, "I won't get caught," or "It can't happen to me." In the end, you can't consistently get away with anything, and if you keep it up and finally trip over the consequences, don't go blaming Saturn for your bad luck, blame yourself. Negligence of responsibilities and ignoring the often obvious consequences of our acts are two characteristics that often reap "bad luck."

Another thing you find out, when you listen to some of these monologues by "unlucky" people, is that their bad luck has a pattern to it that is too blatant to be accidental. What do you say to a woman who had an alcoholic father and has the "bad luck" to marry three men in succession who "turn out to be alcoholics?" Do you say, "You need a lucky charm," or do you say, "You need a shrink"? Patterns like these are not bad luck at all, but neurotic. Psychotherapy or self-analysis of some kind is needed to help the person understand and correct the unconscious need to be involved in such self-defeating behavior. (Understanding the chart can be a good way of getting insight into this kind of problem.)

One component of Jupiter we didn't discuss is the ability to learn from experience, and many "unlucky" people don't seem to be able to do so, even when they are not neurotic. They keep on making the same mistakes over and over and then say, "It's just my bad luck." What is needed sometimes is just to learn the habit of going over such situations in your mind to find out what went wrong. You can then take action to correct it or plan how to handle such situations in the future. Try to really analyze what is going on, and don't pass the buck about your part in it.

In some bad luck, I also find that there is a method to the madness. I worked with unmarried mothers for years, and it was obvious to me that no matter how much they talked about their "bad luck in getting caught," the pregnancy was unconsciously quite deliberate and served many different needs, e.g., the need to retreat from a threatening success that might demand too much of them. Of course, just as there are people who "enjoy ill health," there are people who enjoy their bad luck. They think it makes them a dramatic, tragic figure or entitles them to a little extra attention. There are certain cultures where it gives you quite a bit of status to be this kind of tragic figure. I personally could do without it—I'd rather be quietly, consistently lucky than dramatically unlucky.

Jupiter — Overrated or Not?

In the course of this chapter, we've looked at Jupiter in its many facets, trying to find the underlying connections between them (a typically Jupiterian activity!). We've also considered the elements that make good luck, good fortune, and success—those lovely things attributed to Jupiter traditionally—and we have found that no more luck comes from Jupiter than from Saturn, that both have a role to play in our success if used positively. We've even found that the misuse of Jupiterian energies can bring us as much bad luck as any so-called malefic. What is important in using the Jupiterian energies within us is balance—the same need we've been finding in studying the role of each of the planets in our lives.

CHAPTER 8

TO SATURN, WITH LOVE

Among the hundreds of phobias is a very common one that hasn't made the dictionaries yet, but it will be there as soon as the lexicographers get hip to astrology. I'm talking about *Saturnophobia*, a neurosis that seems to hit only astrologers and their students and clients. However, since this includes a growing number of people, Saturnophobia could some day be the most common mental health problem in America. Saturnophobia, which is simply the fear of Saturn, is not as crippling as claustrophobia, but it does hold back your spiritual growth. If you are still calling Saturn such things as "the greater malefic" or "the grim reaper," you are Saturnophobic. Since knowledge can dispel fear, let's take a good look at what you are afraid of. You may even come around to my position, which is that it is the most benefic of all the planets. I make no bones about it, I'm having a love affair with Saturn.[1]

Saturn's Glyph & Physical Form

Saturn is beautiful to look at. If you've seen it through a telescope, you know that pictures don't do it justice. Its lovely white light, especially, is hard to capture on film. It is interesting to speculate on the metaphysical meaning of Saturn's rings. How can they call it a malefic when it wears a halo? This suggests the tremendous spiritual strength that can come from using your Saturn in a positive way. Occultists talk about the "ring pass not," and I do think Saturn is a spiritual turning point. Until you master Saturn, the planets beyond it—Uranus, Neptune, and Pluto—can give you great difficulty. Saturn viewed from the side, as we usually see it, is ⬭ . If you changed perspectives and saw it from millions of miles above, it would look like this ◉ . That's very much like the glyph for the Sun, and

---

1. This chapter originally appeared in *Astrology Guide*, the 7/77 issue, ©1977, Sterling Publications. It is reprinted with their permission.

I do suspect there is a strong link between Saturn and the Sun. Only as you mature does your real self (Sun) shine through in its fullest strength and development.

Saturn has to do with time, and the rings suggest that time is circular or cyclic, that patterns are always repeating themselves, and that you can't just consider one point in time in making a decision, but must consider everything that went before it and everything that comes after it. This connection between Saturn's rings and time is backed up by the difficulty any astrologer has in talking about Saturn without referring to its cycles and what they mean in your life. A basic rule of architecture is that form follows function, and I guess that must be true of celestial architecture as well, because Saturn's rings have much to do with the function of Saturn in our lives. The recently discovered rings of Uranus also make sense in terms of this theory of celestial architecture, because, after Saturn, the cycles of Uranus seem to be the next most important in marking transitions in the human life cycle. And, the fact that both of them have rings points to a fraternal nature between Saturn and Uranus. Not only have they been considered co-rulers of Aquarius, but their cycles mesh at key ages: around 21, 42, 63, and 84.

Rod Chase has pointed out the significance of Saturn's density. Even though it is 95 times the size of the earth, it is so light that it would float in one of our oceans if we could set it there. He feels this shows that we shouldn't feel burdened down by Saturn and its responsibilities, but should undertake them with a light heart.

The glyph for Saturn is written in several ways, but I suspect the "circle of spirit" addicts of tampering with it to make it fit into their neat pattern. I feel, like many others, that the glyph represents a sickle, and should be written ♄ . I said earlier that it is Saturnophobic to call Saturn "the *grim* reaper," but I do believe it has to do with reaping what you have sown. If you've sown and tilled things that are good for you, then Saturn brings a joyous harvest, and you are rewarded by getting what you richly deserve. If you've sown things that are harmful for you, then Saturn harvests that too. People have this idea of Saturn and of karma as punitive, but it really is just an impersonal principle that works regardless of whether you're putting it to a good or a harmful use. Saturn is *not* out to get you.

Saturn — Plus & Minus

Saturn has many positive traits, and without them we would accomplish very little of lasting worth. I have found it difficult, however, to separate Saturn's traits into lists of positive and negative, because most of the negative uses are only exaggerations of the positive. This is true of all the planets to some extent, but it seems especially true of Saturn. Let me show you what I mean.

In the human body, Saturn rules the skeletal system— the bones, cartilage, and skin which give us our shape and keep us from flopping all over like jellyfish. In our lives, Saturn also has to do with structure and form. How well you are able to organize things and deal with structure is shown by the sign and the aspects of your Saturn. It also shows the type of order which works best for you and the areas where you are most organized. People with Saturn in Gemini may develop an excellent filing system for their papers, because that is their priority, but may not have the faintest idea what's at the bottom of the Fibber McGee's closet in their hall. The person with Saturn in the sixth may be very organized about his work but have trouble keeping track of social engagements. Being *too* organized is a negative Saturnian trait—e.g., the kind of person who compulsively makes a list for everything and then makes a list of all the lists. It is not generally possible to be organized and structured in every area of your life, at least not without sacrificing a great deal of your pleasure and spontaneity in living.

Saturn has to do with rocks and the positive Saturnian is a "rock of Gibraltar"—mature, stable, reliable. They have learned to build their house on a rock, rather than on the sand, knowing things have more permanency when done carefully and with solid foundations. This can be carried to an extreme, of course, and you get the Saturnian who's like your pet rock—too solid, too immovable, and too rigid. Not content with small rocks, Saturn and Capricorn also have to do with mountains, and these people are mountain climbers at heart. Their goals are the heights, and they prepare carefully for their long climb to success, eliminating all that's unnecessary. They are able to plan ahead and set priorities. Naturally, some Saturnians are ambitious to the point of ruthlessness, using people—or climbing right over them—in order to reach their goals. (Saturnians include people with important planets in Capricorn or the tenth house and those with Saturn on the Ascendant or Midheaven or aspecting their Sun or Moon.)

Many Capricornian or Saturnian people have trouble with their knees, the part of the body associated with Capricorn. Since every physical problem has its metaphysical causes, the cause here is lack of flexibility in the personality. Knees have to bend, but the too-rigid Saturnian has trouble bending with the needs of the moment. To get down on your knees is to show humility, and, while the Saturnian can be very self-critical, there is nonetheless a great lack of humility in many of them. ("I may be terribly imperfect, but I'm miles ahead of the rest of you.") Rod Chase has a wonderful motto for Capricorn that says it all, "In order to climb the mountain, you've got to bend your knees."

Self-discipline is an important positive trait we associate with Saturn. Without it, how can we accomplish anything important? Patience, perseverance, and the spartan avoidance of distracting temptations are facets of self-discipline and are all Saturnian virtues too. Again, self-discipline in every area is an impossibility unless you ignore some very human needs and pleasures. Executives who neglect their families for work and more work probably consider themselves admirably self-disciplined, but they are not living a balanced life. Saturn transits, properly used, are great opportunities to increase your self-discipline, not only in the area of the chart involved, but in the core of your being as well. (This chapter on Saturn is being written on a transit of Saturn to my Mars, which many astrologers would consider a very negative and difficult transit. Instead, I've learned ways of disciplining and conserving my energy so the book can be written.)

A primary lesson of Saturn is responsibility. Blaming others for what happens to you is a mark of immaturity. Spiritual teachers and psychotherapists agree that once you have passed childhood, you are responsible for yourself and your actions. If Saturn in your chart is a problem area, sit down and honestly ask yourself, "Am I passing the buck? What is my part in this problem? Where did I neglect my duty to myself and others?" Spiritual teachers tell us it is better to do this on a day-by-day basis, or at least once a year as in the Jewish holiday, Rosh Hashanah, so that you resolve your karma as you go along, rather than be left to do it at the end of life.

People with a strong Saturn often take on heavy responsibilities from a young age... the kind of child who is forced to be an adult. The capacity to accept responsibility, of course, is a prerequisite for success, but the person who can't delegate some of that responsibility to others pays a tremendous personal cost and also robs others of their opportunity to grow and learn. You may feel that others will let you down, but you then have a responsibility to teach and supervise them in fulfilling their tasks.

In psychological language, Saturn is the reality principle. You always have to face up to reality under a Saturn transit, and since most of us prefer to cherish our illusions, this is another reason Saturn is called a "malefic." But reality was always there, and it is your fault, not Saturn's, if you've avoided facing up to it. Positive Saturnians are realistic. . . another reason for their success. They are too practical to invest their energies in something that just won't work out, and they can foresee the consequences of an action because they take a long-range view. They can sometimes be *too* realistic. . . lacking imagination, being first-order wet blankets who are afraid to take a chance, and possibly balancing on that fine dividing line between pragmatism and opportunism. . . but it's just an exaggeration of basically positive traits.

Saturnian people are serious, a characteristic that's not properly valued in our hedonistic society. The youthful Saturnian, especially, is often unappreciated by his peers. Nonetheless, a serious, "take care of business" approach can help you accomplish a great deal. Here, it is easy to overbalance on the negative side and become somber, melancholy, and depressed. Saturnophobia may not be in the dictionary yet, but *saturnine* is, meaning gloomy. Depressive persons are not using their strong Saturns in a positive way. When they start working hard at some goal they consider worthwhile, they stop feeling so sorry for themselves. Likewise, under a Saturn transit, we can be depressed unless we use that time to be serious and work hard on something meaningful.

Perfectionism is a negative trait attributed to Saturn and Capricorn people, but again this is just a positive trait they've gone overboard with. On the positive level, it is a concern with high quality and with doing things to the best of their ability. The most professional people I know are Capricorns—in the positive sense of knowing their business and doing it well. All my personal physicians are Capricorns and I wouldn't have it any other way.

They can be professional in the negative sense of the word too, overly formal, hierarchical, and bound by the traditional ways of doing things. This is why the word professional is an anathema instead of a compliment to today's young people. Also, in their concern for quality and correctness, Saturnians *can* be too perfectionistic with themselves and others. Perfectionism can even get in the way of accomplishment because in compulsively redoing things that are already good enough to be functional, you take up time that could be used to move ahead. Or, you may be so perfectionistic about some endeavor that you are afraid even to try.

Saturn's Cycles & Transits

We spoke earlier about Saturn's rings, associating them with the cycles of Saturn. We won't discuss the cycles in any great detail here, because many other astrologers have done that quite well. Briefly, however, Saturn's cycle around the Sun takes about 28 years, and we become true adults only at about the age when Saturn has completed its first cycle, a period we call the Saturn return. The hard aspects of Saturn (squares and oppositions) take place each seven years, so each 7-year period is closed off by a new phase of maturing and taking stock of our lives.

These are the normal stress periods of living and growing, which psychologists call "normative crises" (e.g., adolescent turmoil at 14 or striking out on your own at 21). We all go through these crises, but if your natal Saturn has difficult aspects, (hard aspects to the Sun, Moon, Ascendant or Neptune, for instance), these periods can be more difficult for you. If you are a Saturnian person, however, you have to live harmoniously with Saturn and put it to good use, so periods like your Saturn return or other Saturn transits are opportunities to work out of the negative uses of Saturn and into the positive.

Saturn has to do with maturing and aging, and the positive Saturnian is a mature person. Saturn is a time marker, but it shouldn't be devastating unless you are only marking time. For those who are growing and developing constantly, aging holds little remorse because you're not getting older, you're getting better. We've noted how young Saturnians are too old for their age and usually not well-liked by their peers. This improves with age, especially as they approach the age where Saturnian things are expected of them because of the responsibilities of a career or family. Also, they are probably more at ease once they begin to find a sense of security and self-worth through their accomplishments, so that some of the negative Saturnian traits such as insecurity and self-condemnation ease off.

Saturn transits force you to face up to reality. . . a *jolt* when you've been fooling yourself about the problems you face. But the positive side of this is that once you've finished emoting about the unfairness of reality and of Saturn, you can then get to work on establishing something more substantial and solid. It may not be as much fun as drifting and dreaming on a pink cloud, but they don't take pink clouds as collateral at the bank. Saturn is the wisdom gained from experience. . . even if you're thick-headed and your alma mater is going to be the School of Hard Knocks.

The negative things that happen to you under a Saturn transit are the results of not using Saturn in a positive way in the first place. If you haven't developed self-discipline, a Saturn transit might mean the loss of something you haven't been disciplined about. Discipline imposed from the outside is meant to push you to develop discipline from within. If you've built your house on the sand, figuratively speaking, a Saturn transit might level the house and make you go back to rebuild more solid foundations. Again, Saturn is not punitive, but an impartial rectification of error—the celestial computer kicking it back for correction because "it does not compute."

Used in a positive way, a Saturn transit can give you the help you need to develop stability, strength of character, self-discipline, and a new ability to organize and structure your life. If you've exercised some of these traits already in the area affected by the transit, then it will be a period of further growth in that area and a reaping of the reward for what you've already sowed.

Saturn — the Pearl in the Oyster

The house and sign placement of Saturn in your natal chart is sometimes a trouble spot where you experience delays and obstacles. This is not a pleasurable experience for anyone, but it is often through meeting and overcoming adversities that we achieve something worthwhile. Demosthenes started off trying to overcome a speech impediment and became a great orator. With hard work, Saturn's placement in your chart can lead to something great.

Another metaphor about Saturn may demonstrate this principle more clearly. I compare Saturn to the grain of sand inside an oyster. It frustrates and irritates the oyster, who probably wonders why it is being singled out this way, until it finally mobilizes its defenses to do something about it. It builds and builds, until it has finally created a lovely pearl. We find the pearl beautiful and valuable, but the oyster may very well consider it a great affliction. So, too, the problems we struggle with which are due to Saturn may feel uncomfortable on a day-to-day basis, but in the long run by working at it we may be building something very fine. Look at your Saturn as a pearl in the making, and you'll work along with it better.

CHAPTER 9

URANUS &
THE DIFFERENT DRUMMER

How dull our lives would be without Uranus! It is the planet that blasts us out of our rut when we are too apathetic or too fearful to make a change. It is also the planet of individuality, the force that keeps us from being monotonous replicas of one another. If Uranus has the reputation of being a malefic, no doubt it is because we all fear change and suspect those who are different.

The Glyph for Uranus—♅

The late Donald Bradley (also known as Garth Allen) believed that Uranus has to do with the birth process, whereby we leave the womb and become separate individuals.[1] Bradley feels the glyph for Uranus symbolizes the birth process. In stylized form it shows the infant, head down, passing through the birth canal)—♅—(. As we grow spiritually, we leave other kinds of wombs behind and become more and more individualized. For example, we associate divorce with Uranus, and divorce often means the two parties, particularly the woman, have to become individuals in their own right.

I also see an upside down Venus in the Uranus symbol ♂ , which again tells us something about Uranus. Venus represents such things as love and beauty, and for it to be upside down is to see them in a different perspective. Uranians (people with Uranus or Aquarius strong in their charts) do have a different idea of beauty than the rest of the world—look at modern art, which tends to be produced by Uranus-attuned people. Venus also has to do with relationships, and Uranians can't go along with the traditional ideal of legalized monogamous heterosexual marriage as their only option in relationships. In the Aquarian Age, in

---

1. Both Pluto and Uranus are connected with the birth, but Pluto is the reproductive process, the gradual growth of something new within you, while Uranus is the expulsion of that new life form into a new environment, and the severing of the connection with the old, as in the cutting of the umbilical cord.

fact, the whole idea of love may have to be turned upside down; impersonal love for all (*agape*) more than possessive personal love may be the key to achieving those Aquarian/ Uranian ideas of universal brotherhood and world peace.

Finally, the glyph reminds me of a person doing a supported headstand, a yoga exercise which improves the flow of blood and oxygen to the brain and helps us become more clear-headed. The Uranian strives always to be clear-headed, but his ideas may sometimes seem upside down to the rest of us. We all have Uranus and Aquarius somewhere in our charts, however, so somewhere in our lives our ideas are contrary to the established norms.

Astronomers use another glyph for Uranus ⊙⃗ and the German astrologers have adopted it. I don't know why astronomers selected that particular glyph, but it appears to be a combination of the Sun ⊙ and Mars ♂ . Does this shed any light on the meaning of Uranus? It is true that only as we gain a sense of who we are ⊙ can our energies be properly directed ♂ , and that happens when we truly become individuals in our own right.

Properties of the Planet Uranus

The glyph for Uranus ♅ looks rather different from the glyphs of other planets, and this alerts us to the fact that Uranus has to do with differentness. The connection of Uranus with differentness is seen again when we learn about the physical properties of the planet Uranus itself. The book *Astronomy Made Simple* points out four ways that Uranus is unique.[2] All four seem to me to be related to the meaning of Uranus.

In the first place Uranus is unique in that it was the first planet to be discovered with the aid of a telescope. This seems appropriate, as Uranus has to do with technology and the development of modern science. Second, Uranus was discovered by accident while William Herschel, an amateur astronomer, was making other observations.[3]

2. Meir Degani, *Astronomy Made Simple*, Doubleday 1966, p. 163.
3. Uranus' rings, the astronomical surprise of 1977, were also discovered by accident. That discovery revived the plans for the Voyager's exploration of the outer planets, which had been shelved.

Uranus has to do with accidents, both accidents to the physical body and accidents in the creative process (as in Eureka!). It is also typical that Uranus was revealed first to an amateur rather than to the scientific establishment— Uranus is an antiestablishment force in our lives. Third, Uranus rotates "backwards" on its axis, at least when compared with the rest of the planets, and Uranian people want to set themselves in opposition to the ordinary way of doing things.

Finally, Uranus is sideways, its equator forming almost a right angle to its orbit around the sun. Diagramed, it would look like this-⦶-whereas the other planets would look like this ⊖. The right angle in astrology is a *square* —a conflict aspect—and Uranians are perpetually in conflict with society. If the Sun is the center of our being as well as the center of the solar system, then, to have Uranus at right angles to its orbit around the Sun, suggests both a positive and negative interpretation. In order to become true individuals, we must at some points be in conflict with what appears to be the accepted path or norm, and we must also take a look at our own progress from different perspectives. On the other hand, if we are perpetually in conflict for its own sake, we lose our perspective and are no longer centered.

In these four ways, the planet Uranus is the rule-breaker of astronomy, and Uranian people believe that rules are made to be broken. In another solar system, however, Uranus might be the rule rather than the exception—that is, in some solar systems, all planets might rotate "backwards" and "sideways." Likewise, what is considered odd or different about Uranian people in our society may well be the norm somewhere else.

The Process of Individuation

Let us return now to Donald Bradley's remarkable insight that the glyph for Uranus represents birth, with its trauma of separating from the womb, but also with the accompanying freedom to become a more separate individual. Psychoanalytical thinkers like Erik Erikson and Erich Fromm call this repeated happening at various stages and levels of our lives *individuation*—that is, the process of becoming more and more an individual in your own right. Individuation is inevitable to some degree in every life, however involuntary it may be. Many of us are afraid to leave the womb—the safe but confining family circle, the secure but boring job, the limited but familiar patterns of thought. In his book, *Escape From Freedom*, Fromm talks about this fear of striking out on our own and relates it not only to the problems of the individual but also to society's problems, such as the rise of Nazism.

Uranian people (and also those under a Uranus transit) have no choice but to strike out on their own—they are impelled to action by a restlessness, a creative itch, and a discomfort with what *is*. They are pushed to greater and greater individuation, through more and more ethereal but no less difficult birth canals. The greater the individuation, however, the more such a person stands out against the conforming masses and the more vulnerable he becomes to society's fear of the person who is different. It is a lonely position. As Fromm points out, the higher the pinnacle of individuation, the greater the corresponding urge to blend back into the safe comforting crowd. Thus, not only is the Uranian in perpetual conflict with society, but also in constant conflict with the self-protective shell of the self (Saturn).

Since the loneliness and vulnerability of the Uranian are acutely painful, a common solution is the formation of some sort of in-group with people who share the same ideals and problems. While this group may be actively opposed to the conformity forced on us by society, an even more intimidating pressure to conform usually develops within the group itself. Once more, there is an escape from freedom into something that can be more confining than the society they rebelled against. The in-group leaders are sometimes more dictatorial than any of the authorities they oppose. Naturally, this is rationalized as necessary to the success of the common cause. We can observe the tendency to form in-groups in many kinds of Uranians—from teenagers, to creative people of various sorts, to active radicals, all the way to astrologers themselves.

In-Groups: Teens, Rebels & Radicals

If you are surprised that I include teenagers in the list above, remember that adolescence is a period of rebellion. Teenagers' clothing, speech, customs, and behavior are all very different from what the adult world expects or desires. Requests and demands made by their parents and teachers are balked at simply because of the source. The peer group—going along with the crowd—is what is important to the teen. If the current fad dictates that they wear their clothes inside out, that's what they will do. Anyone who deviates from the ever-changing norm is pressured to conform, and, if they can't or won't blend in, they are cruelly ostracized. (Likewise, counter-revolutionaries are "purged.")

Is living through adolescence just an unpleasant occupational hazard for teens and their parents, or does this period serve some constructive purpose? Fromm and Erikson believe it is a crucial phase of individuation, in which young persons free themselves of dependency on parents and begin to learn how to function independently. All Uranian movements and transitions are likely to be extremist at first, until the new development is firmly established and accepted, when it can then take on a milder form. Thus, the teen has to rebel hard at first to establish his or her freedom and independence. Many parents need this kind of shock in order to wake up to the fact that they are no longer dealing with a child. Often, though, the need for rebellion comes from inside the teen rather than because of anything imposed from the outside. The teen has to struggle against dependency needs and against the image of the parent lodged inside. For unless this stage is successfully mastered, you can get the eternally dependent child of 40 who never left home. The stronger the Uranus in the birth chart, the stronger may be the period of adolescent rebellion. If it is any comfort to the parent or teen going through it, charts such as these show tremendous creative potential or some particular role to play in righting the things that are wrong with our society. A soul of this type would need an unusual degree of freedom and independence to achieve the things it came in for.

The question of what makes a rebel or radical is a complex one. Certainly, a strong Uranus would be a predisposing factor, but we all have Uranus in our chart, and under the right circumstances, we could all be induced to rebel. For the common man, the period around the French and American Revolutions was a time of revolt; not coincidentally, Uranus was discovered in 1781. Women, students, blacks, and gay people have felt sufficiently oppressed in recent years to start revolts of their own. The career radical, however, has a strong Uranus (and often a strong Neptune). Perhaps Uranians do not start off rebellious, only different. Like the sidewise planet that rules them, their perspective on life, their ideas, desires, and behavior do not fit the established pattern. When their non-conformity results in oppression and ostracism, the behavior takes on a note of defiance, and thus is perpetuated. They can become radicalized partly in self-defense, standing up for their right to be different, and partly out of anger that society should try to force them into a mold that is not of the individual's making.

I looked up the word radical in the dictionary and found that its original meaning was "going to the roots, or fundamental."[4] (*Radical* comes from *radix,* meaning *root,* and radicals often talk about "grass roots movements" or "grass roots democracy.") The word has subsequently taken on the meaning of favoring extreme changes or reforms, and it is true that radicals recommend getting at the very roots of problems, which would mean making some very fundamental changes in our society. (Astrologers are Uranian too, and it tickles me to hear them talk about

---

4. *Thorndike Barnhart Comprehensive Desk Dictionary,* p. 640. (1965 Edition)

"radical charts." To an astrologer, however, a radical chart is not the horoscope of a revolutionary, but the *root* or birth horoscope to which progressions and transits are applied).

Radicals will generally try to band together in the kind of in-group we discussed earlier. Forming an organized, structured group of Uranians, however, is almost an impossibility. They are individualistic and can't accept the authority of a group of their peers any better than they could accept the authority of the establishment. Fierce in-fighting ultimately develops, and finally a faction will break off and form a *splinter* group. (How Uranian that term is!). The energy that could go toward the cause is often expended on this type of in-fighting. The effectiveness of many of the movements of recent years has been limited by the participants' inability to agree on a particular course of action for any sustained length of time.

Uranus & Astrology

Uranus is the planet designated by the majority of astrologers as having to do with astrology, and most astrologers seem to have both Uranus and Neptune strong in their charts. Needless to say, that makes them difficult individuals to deal with. Not You and I, mind you, but "those other astrologers" tend to be eccentric, dogmatic, contrary, and elitist! Trying to keep an astrology organization together and functioning harmoniously is like trying to get a union of anarchists to agree. Each astrologer has his own viewpoint, and, rather than recognize that as a necessary and even desirable consequence of their Uranian nature, they insist that those who do not agree with them are "the enemy." Feuds are commonplace, and, as a result, astrology has more warring splinter groups than the New Left. There is even a faction who call themselves Uranian astrologers. At first I thought the term a pure redundancy, but later found it applied to the techniques they use.

Uranus rules Aquarius, so the Age of Aquarius should see astrology become a prominent part of our lives. Popular astrology, dealing with Sun signs alone, is becoming increasingly familiar to the masses. While many astrologers deride this as superficial, nonetheless I feel it is a step forward. Our society has not been an introspective one, and I see Sun Sign astrology as the beginning of a mass desire to look into and understand the self. Naturally, the more introspective person will progress beyond the Sun Sign level into the deeper levels of self-awareness an individual chart can provide.

Astrology, being Uranian, carries all the danger of Uranian excess. The New Age prejudice could easily be along Sun Sign lines rather than by race or creed. Uranians are notoriously detached, and another danger is that we will use astrology and its technical jargon to *detach* ourselves from our emotions and the reality of things that happen to us. (To be too detached is to be schizoid, which happens with some Uranian people.) We can also easily use astrology to detach ourselves from our personal responsibility for the things that happen to us. ("It was Neptune that caused me to drink, Judge.") Hopefully, we will eventually learn to use that Uranian detachment in the more positive sense— by using astrology to gain a new perspective on ourselves and our problematic behavior and helping us to discover our own individuality.

Genius & Eccentricity

I heard that someone once did a survey and found that there were more Aquarians in the Hall of Fame than any other sign. I also heard that someone else did a survey of a mental hospital and also found more Aquarians there than any other sign. I can't swear to the truth of either story, but it certainly smacks of that old saying about the fine line between genius and insanity.

Whether the Uranian winds up in the Hall of Fame or the looney bin is often, once more, a matter of society and its definitions of our behavior. If the Uranian, with that different perspective, comes up with insights, ideas, and discoveries which are useful, interesting, or entertaining to that particular culture in that particular era, then society will say that person is a genius. On the other hand, if the ideas, discoveries, and insights are not seen as useful or entertaining in a way *that* particular society is prepared to understand and use, then the person is defined as eccentric. Same individual—different label. When the society changes, the definition of the Uranian individual may also change. Prophets are without honor in their own country, and many brilliant, creative people have to separate from their original birthplace in order to be appreciated and acclaimed. Likewise, many geniuses are ahead of their time—considered crackpots in their own era and not recognized until decades or even centuries later. Society imposes its labels on us, and the labels are often wrong.

Like other Uranians, creative and brilliant individuals are often ostracised because they are different. Again, like other Uranians, they create their own in-groups—writers' clubs, artists' collectives, Mensa, and the like. In so far as these groups foster and nurture the individuality of the artist, they are a great source of comfort, inspiration, and fellowship. They can, sometimes, fall into the pitfall of other in-groups by dictating conformity of style and, in such cases, can be counter-productive.

We have talked as though genius and creativity were the property of an elite, but astrology should immediately show the fallacy of that line of thought. Uranus has to do with genius, and we all have Uranus and Aquarius in our charts, so we all have our own particular brand of genius in some area of our lives. Society, by discouraging non-conformity, stifles our creativity and also defines genius along very narrow lines—the fine arts, academia, and science. If it doesn't fit into those categories, we don't recognize it. A thorough understanding of your chart can help you to tap into your personal genius.

Uranus and You

It keeps sounding like I'm talking about "they" and "them" instead of *me* and *you* when I'm talking about

Uranians. That shows how deeply we are conditioned to view people in terms of in-groups and out-groups and how far we are from the Aquarian ideal of universal brother/sisterhood. There is no such thing as an average person, no such thing as normal. These are illusions based on statistics and on our tendency to hide anything within ourselves that seems different. We all have Uranus and Aquarius somewhere in our charts, and so we all have our "kinks" and "quirks." Strangely enough, if we participate in group experiences like sensitivity groups, encounter groups, consciousness-raising groups, or self-help groups, we find that these seeming quirks are not so strange after all, but shared by many people. It is only because of the rigidity and morality of our society's condemnations that people do not freely speak of these things. Groups are considered Uranian or Aquarian, perhaps because such experiences, detached from our daily lives, do raise our consciousness and give us a sense of brother/sisterhood with others. We are then faced with a paradox. . . and what could be more Uranian than a paradox? On the one hand, it is often in groups that we can see our own particular uniqueness shine through, by its contrast with other people, but it is also in groups that we can feel the deep bond of common human-ness we share with all people. In other words, we each do have uniqueness, but we're also still bonded by our common humanity.

Astrology, a Uranian discipline, can also help to relieve our feeling of estrangement from humanity and yet at the same time affirm our individuality. (We all contain all the planets and all twelve signs and houses, so we do have basic needs and emotions in common with everyone else; yet the particular combination of house and sign placements and aspects to planets is unique, so we, too, are unique.) When practiced by an astrologer who is free of society's brainwashing and who can view your chart without judgement, astrology can help you see yourself in a new perspective, free of the labels and "shoulds" society has imposed on you. Both astrology and group experiences are Uranian, and when used in a balanced way, both can bring about a healing of the Uranian problems of feeling isolated and ostracized because of our differences. This is a homeo-pathic approach, an idea I have been developing for some time. The *homeopathic* system of medicine is one where a cure is brought about by applying some of the same sort of substance that caused the problem. (The closest equivalent in traditional or *allopathic* medicine is vaccination, whereby we develop immunity to certain diseases.) In astrology, I see it as identifying a problem as being related to the Uranus or Saturn or Pluto parts of ourselves (or any other part) and undertaking a remedy which is related to the same planet. For example, the Saturnian problems of depression and anxiety can sometimes be relieved by the Saturnian remedy of self-discipline and hard work.

Accidents & Breaks Under Uranus Transits

When a client is having a Uranus transit, the astrologer will generally warn against accidents. This is not the only possibility, but certainly it is wise to be cautious. Perhaps we should take a look at accidents and see how they come about. My metaphysics teacher, Eric Pace, once linked acci-dents and rebellion without knowing that both are ruled by Uranus. The person who has an accident is usually rebelling against safety rules, and many Uranians are accident prone. Uranians believe that rules are made to be broken—but unfortunately, so are arms, legs, and ankles. At a deeper level, however, if we could study it more closely, I think we'd find that most self-caused accidents come about during a flare-up of rebellious feelings. During a field trip my writ-ing class went on recently, I had two potentially serious accidents in the space of an hour. I knew exactly what was going through my mind each time, because we were in-structed to observe our feelings and thoughts while doing certain things. Each time, the accident immediately followed a flare-up of rebelliousness at having to follow instructions. You may want to observe this in yourself after even a minor accident—try to reconstruct what you were thinking about immediately before.

After many serious accidents, however, people suffer a curious amnesia and can't remember what happened. This is attributed to "shock" (a Uranian word), and that may be partially true. Most amnesia and forgetting, however, have a large component of repression, which involves shoving unacceptable wishes and emotions into the unconscious. What could be unacceptable about a self-caused accident, except the motivation behind it? At the unconscious level, there is no such thing as an accident—many are unconsciously carefully arranged. The motive may be a rebellious one ("I will subvert their demands by hurting myself"), a self-destructive one, or even a desperate attempt to escape some situation. Nonetheless, there *is* a motivation behind the accidents we cause ourselves.

Not all accidents are negative—the physical results are undesirable—but if the accident leads the person to new understanding of what she is rebelling against, it can lead to positive change. For example, one of my friends was living in a communal farm arrangement that she had become very unhappy about but could see no way out of. For her, the way out took the form of breaking her leg—twice. After the second break, her parents came and took her home, she went into therapy, and ultimately went to school to become a chiropractor. The accidents were a turning point in her life, even though the pain and suffering were considerable. However, had she known herself well enough to break away from a situation that stifled her individuality, an accident in which she broke her leg would not have been necessary.

Uranus seems to have a great deal to do with breaks. (Saturn, on the other hand, is *brakes*.) Under Uranus transits couples may "break up." Some people have "break downs"—which are not always mentally unhealthy when they cause us to "break away" from or change situations which are destructive. Teenagers "break out" in pimples— all skin conditions metaphysically represent an identity problem, and Uranus has to do with the search for one's individuality. Not all breaks are negative. When creative or inventive "accidents" and discoveries occur, we call that a "break through" or a "lucky break." When a Uranus transit occurs and you have an accident, it should be a signal that your unconscious is asking you to break away from something that is stifling your individuality and causing you to rebel. Give yourself a break and analyze what that situation is.

The Uranus Transit — Lightning Bolt or Earthquake?

I have often heard a Uranus transit described as "a bolt out of the blue"—a completely unexpected event that strikes like lightning. When you look more deeply, however, a great deal was going on under the surface long before the event. Uranus and the birth process go back to Bradley's metaphor—that baby didn't just appear out of the blue; it was growing in the womb for nine months. Therefore, I don't agree that Uranus transits are like a bolt of lightning; they are more like an earthquake. Earthquakes can also seem like a bolt out of the blue, but the process leading up to one can teach us a great deal about Uranus. Deep under the surface of the earth, there are long jagged cracks in the rock layers which are called faults. (Significantly, they can be shaped like the glyph for Aquarius ♒). If the edges of the crack are poorly aligned, tension and pressure build up along the fault until it suddenly gives and creates an earthquake. Then there is a series of after-*shocks*—as various parts of the fault realign themselves in compensation and settle into place.

Uranus transits may operate in a similar way. A split or schism can develop underground in our lives which would be similar to a fault. Perhaps your marriage is stifling your individuality, and you begin to want your freedom. Pressure continues to build up, until a Uranus transit signals a separation or the need for marital counseling to work out innovative (Uranian) approaches to the relationship that make more freedom and individuality possible for both. In this example, the "after-shocks" are the adjustments you and your spouse have to make afterwards.

Pressure along a fault is a metaphor that can account for much of the unexpected or unpredictable behavior people exhibit with a Uranus transit. People who suddenly leave a successful career to go live in the mountains probably have yearned for years to break away from the pressure of that kind of work. Sudden acts of violence are sometimes seen under Uranus transits—they are sometimes the unleashing of years of stored up anger and frustration. An argument may be helpful in clearing away the tension between two people.

Are these kinds of earthquakes necessary in our lives? No, if you don't allow that much pressure to build up along the fault. A fault that is not earthquake-prone is one with a good deal of "slippage"—that is, flexibility. Don't repress your individuality and your need for some freedom to the point of self-destruction. The more rigidly you adhere to a set of social mores that try to force you to be what you aren't, the more pressure will build up along the fault—and the bigger that earthquake will have to be to put your life in its proper alignment.

Uranus & Crisis

Shock is a Uranian word. Electricity shocks us if we are not properly grounded—and we also behave in shocking ways when we are not grounded, i.e., centered. *Shock* therapy is an extreme treatment for mental illness, and sometimes we need a great shock in our lives in order to jolt us out of our inertia. Donald Bradley says that Uranus is the planet of progress through shock, as it startles us out of our complacency.

Many people seem to have a real need to create crisis. Not only is it more exciting (Uranus is electric), but often a crisis is the only way we know of to get moving. This is partly due to our own inertia and resistance to change—sometimes we need that heightened emotion and awareness to motivate us. It is also partly due to social pressure against change—people around us don't like the status quo disturbed either and will put a lot of pressure on us not to rock the boat. As a result, we often unconsciously create a crisis which will be deemed sufficient cause for the desired change. The woman or man, for instance, who has a good home and a nice family but just doesn't love their spouse any more, will have a hard time breaking away unless some dramatic event occurs (e.g., falling in love with someone else or provoking physical violence). Or you may have a secure, lucrative job that bores you to tears. If you quit for something insecure and less lucrative but more exciting, people will demand an explanation—"Why did you do that? You had a perfectly good job." Getting fired solves the problem—it appears not to be your own choice.

There are such strong social pressures to conform and thus to repress real self-expression and individuality, that we feel we have to have a reason or an excuse to break away from the things that keep us from being ourselves. A Uranus transit is often that kind of explosion, that kind of crisis that gives us permission to make the change we've been wanting a long time but didn't have the courage to make. The only problem is, change and crisis that is imposed from the outside is often painful and destructive. Why break a leg—why not just break away? Or take a break, now and then? The courage to be who you are comes from Uranus— doing a bit of your own Uranian thing everyday will keep the more destructive effects of Uranus from being necessary.

CHAPTER 10
LIVING WITH NEPTUNE —
THE TIDE CAN'T ALWAYS BE IN

It is remarkable how often my current moods or circumstances mirror the planet I am writing or teaching about. Classes on Mercury or Gemini are full of sidetracks, jokes, and lively discussions, while classes on Saturn are dead serious. Never has this principle been so true as in writing this chapter on Neptune, which has taken NINE months. (Nine is Neptune's number.) Neptune is hazy and mysterious; the folder containing my material on Neptune has twice completely disappeared for months at a time. In true Neptunian fashion, I took that as an omen I wasn't meant to write the chapter yet. Neptune is nebulous and disorganized, and another reason this chapter has taken so long is because I haven't had a clue on how to structure it, even though I usually have no trouble organizing my writing.

It's not really surprising that I find myself all at sea on this topic—Neptune was the god of the sea, and the planet Neptune has powerful connections with the ocean. Fish are a symbol for Pisces, which Neptune rules, and also for Christianity, a major religion of the Piscean age. The primeval force of the ocean holds a special fascination for Neptunian people, soothing and calming them. High tides and low ebbs mark the rhythm of our lives, but the Neptunian can spend a lifetime—or several—learning to accept the reality that the tide can't always be in. During low ebbs, Neptunians may seek chemical substances (more Neptune) to get them "high" again, but too much reliance on artificial means, and they can get "hooked". . . start drinking like fish, for instance.

The Material vs. the Astral Plane

A sound footing in reality is necessary in order to deal with life on our material plane, and I'm sure we wouldn't be here if there weren't valuable things for us to learn from it. The Neptunian, however, often wants to cut loose the moorings of this plane and drift and dream. This is true of the addictive personality; it is true of the schizophrenic; and it is true of the medium or mystic. These three types, I maintain, are really one—all Neptunians, but with some differences in what they are "hooked" on.

The proof of this is in the frequency with which Neptunians shift from one hook to another. Many psychics drink heavily or smoke grass to enhance their perceptions. Alcoholics join A.A., which is a deeply religious and spiritual experience, and many drug addicts have been cured by conversion to Christianity. A study financed by the National Institute of Drug Abuse showed that nearly half of all heroin addicts are alcoholics or have severe drinking problems.[1] A number of psychiatrists have noted how uncannily psychic their patients are, and religious delusions are common among psychotics. In certain groups, such as the Puerto Rican spiritualist cult, folks that you and I might regard as crazy are looked on as possessed by spirits and revered as messengers of God.[2] Does it make you uncomfortable to tie crazies, drunks and junkies together with "spiritually enlightened people" like you and me? Like it or not, Neptune is a strong factor in all these paths.[3] We've all got Neptune to deal with and there, as they say in A.A., but for the grace of God, go you and I. The battle is not won once for all time, either; to maintain sound mental health when engaged in spiritual pursuits, you must constantly strive to deal with Neptune in a balanced way.

What is the common thread between these seemingly different groups? I believe it is an unusual attachment to the astral plane, where we all go nightly in dreams and where we return after death. For those who may not consciously be familiar with it, the astral plane is a non-material state of existence where our thoughts and emotions immedi-

1. This study, done at the Eagleville, Pa. Hospital and Rehabilitation Center, was reported in the National Enquirer on 1/25/77, p. 34.

2. An interesting article on that subculture appeared in the American Journal of Sociology in the early 1960's: Lloyd H. Rogler & August B. Hollingshead, "The Puerto Rican Spiritualist as a Psychiatrist."

3. This is derived from the traditional view in astrology. Currently, Robert Knight and I are embarked on a large research project to test the true astrological correlations of alcohol and drug addiction.

ately assume apparent reality. It lacks the boundaries of time and space which govern our material plane, so the psychically awakened are able, through astral travel, to move forward or backward in time or to see what is happening in distant places. (I prefer to say psychically awakened, because all of us have psychic ability, however latent. For most of us, a strong physical or emotional stress, such as a brush with death or impending danger, may be needed to jar us onto that plane.)

I'm convinced that both psychics and schizophrenics are operating on the astral plane, but the psychic has some ability to do so at will, while the schizophrenic has no choice in the matter and is trapped there, as in a bad dream you cannot break out of. Perhaps the person who claims to be "flying" is actually having an out-of-body experience (i.e., astral traveling). The astral may also play a part in the addictions. Certainly the "trips" and visions of a person on LSD as well as the hallucinations of an alcoholic in D.T.'s must be astrally based.

Even though we all go there nightly in dreams, the astral plane is awesome to most newcomers on the spiritual path, perhaps due to the difficulty in achieving conscious control over it. This fear serves to keep us from attempting psychic feats or astral travel until we are sufficiently mature to deal with them. I'd venture to guess that most bad psychic experiences are given us for the express purpose of warning us off until we are ready for them. A great deal of spiritual maturity is needed to control the emotions, fears, and urges that arise on the astral and also to deal with psychic material in a responsible way. Too many use these things to enhance their ego or to give them some sort of power over others. In either case, the psychic abilities often go sour and unreliable, so the person is tempted to boost them by artificial or fraudulent means. Many mediums who were perfectly genuine in the beginning wind up as frauds when their egos become too involved.

The ego of the negative Neptunian psychic, astrologer, spiritual seeker, or "guru" is often boundless. To be one with God is, of course, the ultimate aim of all spiritual pursuits, but the Neptunian on an ego trip believes he is one with God in some special way . . . like being his "only begotten" son or daughter, an avatar or savior of some sort. So many Neptunians have made me party to this, their most precious innermost secret, that I am now ready to propose a principle to you: SHOW ME A NEPTUNIAN WHO DOESN'T SECRETLY BELIEVE HE'S THE SAVIOR, AND I'LL SHOW YOU A NEPTUNIAN WHO'S LYING!! (Naturally, now that I've gotten so enlightened, I no longer believe I'm *that* important, but I do cherish a persistent and admittedly bizarre notion that I can achieve perfection in this lifetime and not have to incarnate any more.) Doctors, another group of Neptunians, also like to regard themselves as God-like. Significantly, doctors have the highest rate of alcoholism of any profession, perhaps because they are constantly exposed to ego-deflating reminders that they are really only human.

Why should the ego pose such a trap for Neptunians? Astrologer Robert Knight and others designate Neptune as our tie to the collective consciousness, which is our unity with everything that is. Only by forgetting our separateness momentarily can we experience that unity and be one with God. This ecstatic experience of oneness, of merging with something greater than ourselves, is the real HIGH. To focus attention on the ego is not only to lose the high but also to lose touch with the collective consciousness through which psychic connectedness works.

Drug and alcohol users try to create that high artificially—either not knowing or not accepting that it is a transcendence of self through a spiritual experience that they are looking for. Karl Marx said that religion was the opiate of the masses; in an era when the masses no longer find much solace in traditional religion, more and more people are trying to achieve that oneness by opiates and other artificial means. This point was clearly stressed by former Senator Harold Hughes of Iowa, who was an alcoholic before entering politics and has now left politics to become a lay minister. (He was a strong spiritual force in Washington during the Watergate era.) In a radio interview, he was asked to what he attributed the rise of alcoholism and drug addiction in our country. He said it was due to a widespread feeling of *spiritual emptiness*.[4] For people with a strong emphasis on Neptune in their charts, our society's atmosphere of spiritual emptiness can be the most devastating. These people therefore must put extra effort into the search for meaning in life, otherwise the alternative is negative escapism. If they succeed in their task, Neptunian people can become effective teachers, helping to lead people away from the negative Neptunian pursuits and revitalizing people's faith in something that goes far deeper than the material plane we're most familiar with.

Watch Out for Side Effects

Side effects seem to be a peculiarly Neptunian phenomenon. Rest assured that any trumpeted panacea—from the newest medication to the latest idea in social reform—is bound to have unexpected side effects. Today's miracle drug is often tomorrow's headache. In our eagerness to find a solution for some ill, we deceive ourselves about the true nature of the remedy. This principle has been demonstrated repeatedly. Birds or insects introduced from another area to prey on native insects often multiply wildly, due to the lack of their own natural enemies. Eventually they become pests because once their original prey is gone, they turn to wildlife they weren't intended to destroy. This is what happened when rabbits were introduced in Australia. Due to the principle of the survival of the fittest, a stronger remedy often does nothing more than escalate the problem. We are developing stronger and stronger antibiotics that only result in stronger and stronger germs. Stronger and stronger poisons are only creating better cockroaches and the superrat. Similarly, in the addictions, stronger and stronger doses are required as the body develops tolerance.

---

4. Heard on Lutheran Vespers, WFME, N.Y., on 5/30/76. A copy of the entire interview is available on request from Lutheran Vespers, Box 15051, Minneapolis, Minnesota 55415.

The history of addictive drugs in this country shows a similar pattern. Opium was widely hailed as a panacea and used in all kinds of patent medicines in the last century, before people became aware of its addictive properties. Morphine and heroin, successive derivations of opium, also deceived the public at first about their addictive side effects. When heroin addiction became a major social problem, still another opium derivative, methadone, was celebrated as a treatment. What is becoming clear now is that methadone addiction is far more devastating to the body than heroin. In my opinion, it is also a pseudo-treatment in that most methadone clinics do nothing but dispense the drug, rather than attempt any psychotherapy. It is basically a form of social control to keep the addict cool, just as alcohol was used quite consciously by the white man to control the Indian and the black man.

Addiction itself is a side effect of the desire to get high and escape your troubles. Alcohol combines a sedative and an irritant. The kicker is that the sedative effect of one shot lasts only two hours, while the irritating effect on the body lasts 12 hours. Two shots will sedate the body for four hours, but irritate it for 24. Alcohol depresses anxiety and other unpleasant emotions while you are high, but the anxiety level becomes even more pronounced when the alcohol wears off. Thus the alcohol abuser continues to drink to stave off the unpleasant emotions and physical effects. Tolerance builds up over time, and full-fledged alcohol addiction eventually ensues. The alcoholic works hard, however, to convince both self and others that this is not happening, using the Neptunian defense mechanism of *denial* to protect their habit.[5] To seek a panacea to a problem of any kind is to leave yourself open to self-deception and side effects. We lunge at a remedy, like a drowning swimmer at a piece of board, only to find it's really a shark's fin. Another ocean metaphor my Piscean friend Rod Chase uses is "beware of the undertow" that alcohol and other such substances have when we let ourselves be hooked by them.

5. This and other material on alcoholism was derived from an excellent course given by the Bedford-Stuyvesant Alcohol Treatment Center in Brooklyn. People living in the New York City area are able to participate in the course, which is free.

In general, the side effects of escaping your problems is that they get worse. This would be like a garden that has gotten weedy. You decide you just "can't face it," so you leave it alone a week or two. The weeds don't go away; they grow rapidly, getting harder and harder to eradicate. They develop stickers, tendrils, rough leaves, massive roots and tough, woody stalks so that they're really hard to pull. Soon they start taking some of your good plants along with them. If you had pulled them when they were young and tender, it would have been much easier. . . routine drudgery, to be sure, but easier in the long run. Also, with a weed, you have to pull it up whole or it'll grow back from whatever little pieces you left. The big problems we face in life require as much cultivation as a garden.

Should all panaceas be suspected of having negative side effects? I'd say yes, until proven otherwise. Alcohol appears to remove your troubles, and the disease of alcoholism can take many years to develop. The damaging effects of some medicines in use for 20 years and longer are only now being recognized. Likewise, some of the seemingly "spiritual" teachers we so blindly follow can fool us and themselves, and only a long period of observation and testing can prove their merit. We should never accept a single idea without thinking it through for ourselves. Just as overdependence on any chemical substance can lead to physical and emotional imbalance, so, in a similar way, blind, slavish devotion to a human teacher can be a Neptunian trip leading to mental and spiritual imbalance.

Neptune's Pitchfork — Can You Balance on the Middle Tine?

So far we've mostly looked at the negative sides of Neptune, and it seems true that there's more quicksand along the path of Neptune than any other. Neptune brings out the best and the worst in us—the saint and the scoundrel. But what is the good side of Neptune? Perhaps we can understand it by thinking about its relationship to Venus, of which Robert Knight recently reminded me. Neptune is said to be the *higher octave* of Venus, i.e., what Venus would be if carried to its highest possible usage. Venus is personal love and relatedness, and Neptune carries love onto a spiritual level—selfless love, not asking anything in return. It is selfless in that the boundaries of self are dissolved and we are again in the collective consciousness where everything is one. In such a state of psychic attunement, your pain is mine, and identification, compassion (*feeling with*), and sympathy are the natural results.

Balance is again a problem. It is hard to partake of another's pain without becoming enmeshed in it—being dragged so deeply into the problem that you lose perspective and can't help. It is tricky—you have to be separate enough to be objective, yet the Neptunian state negates separateness. The Golden Rule says, "Do unto others as you'd have them do unto you," but if you are over-identified with another person, you often act unwisely, confusing the issue for them and for yourself.

Altruism is a supposed trait of Neptunians and is perhaps a logical extension of Venusian sharing and consideration for others. A Neptunian (or twefth house) dedication to serving the ill and unfortunate can contain a degree of altruism, but as a motivation it is over-rated. The truth is that we gain and learn a great deal from the things we do for others—I'd go so far as to say we always get more than we give in such exchanges. It also makes you feel good and very special—a great boost to the ego. If you watch them closely, there's a heavy streak of egotism in most of the so-called "selfless, altruistic" people among us, even if it masquerades behind a "humbler than thou" facade.

Harmony is attributed to Venus, and music to Neptune. There is no doubt music has a powerful emotional impact. I feel it is one of the ways we become connected with the astral plane, particularly through hymns and chants. I once heard a beautiful quote from the Zohar—"There are halls in the heavens above that open but to the voice of song." If this is true, why do so many jazz and rock and roll musicians become addicted to drugs or alcohol? It is again a shift from one Neptunian hook to another. I feel music must induce a spiritual yearning in them, but they fail to recognize it as such and turn to the chemical pathways to that high-producing unity with all. A popular phrase among musicians several years ago seemed to express this cosmic connection. When they were feeling particularly good, they would say, "Everything is everything."

The good side of Neptune, then, is a vastly improved version of the more personally-concerned Venus. The one characteristic Neptune lacks that belongs to Venus is the principle of *balance*. Neptunians are particularly prone to imbalance—mental, emotional, and spiritual. Until balance is learned, Neptune is not likely to be a truly positive influence in our lives. Under the right circumstances, anyone can slide so easily from the positive side of Neptune to the negative, that it is well to keep in mind that old poem:

> There's so much good in the worst of us
> And so much bad in the best of us
> That it ill behooves any of us
> To pass judgment on the rest of us.

Neptune Transits — Why Me, Lord?

It is very hard to see Neptune as a positive force in our lives, because too often Neptune transits feel anything but positive while they are in process. We are in a fog, confused and deceived by ourselves and others. We are prone to delusions, to excesses and even to breaks with reality. We feel listless, apathetic, depressed, and (inevitably) sorry for ourselves. Time and money disappear, we know not where. Many astrologers seem to think that Neptune teaches only by negative example—i.e., that we must learn to control or avoid the tendencies described above. I think, however, that problems like these are only failures or misfires in our attempts to reach through to the positive side of Neptune. What, then, is the purpose of Neptune in our lives? What is the lesson it can teach us?[6]

6. Parts of this material on Neptune transits appeared in two articles: a. "Get Help from the Outer Planets if You're Facing Big Changes in Your Life," Your Personal Astrology, 7/74, and b. "A Spiritual-Psychological Approach to Transits," Dell Horoscope, 9-10/75.

One day as I sat seeking clarification of these questions I suddenly became aware that the radio was playing "The Impossible Dream." Yes, that *is* one of the functions of Neptune—to raise our sights, to inspire us, to help us dare to dream. Martin Luther King inspired millions with his speech, "I have a dream." Many inspirations and creative ideas come to us under Neptune, even though we may lack the clarity of vision and the determination to carry it through until after the transit is over. But without the inspiration of great dreams, your world would never change. One of my favorite quotes, by Ida Lupino, demonstrates this function clearly. She said, "All of us are standing in the mud, but some of us are reaching for the stars."[7]

My belief about Neptune is that its many manifestations come out of just one universal urge or need—to transcend the bonds of self-hood and merge with something greater. Some of the ways we try to do this are positive and creative, leading us to greater spiritual development, while others just create more of the very problems we are trying to escape. If the negative way is taken during a Neptune transit, at the very least the person learns that what they have chosen is not the right way. We cannot and should not judge another person's spiritual progress or karma from their outward behavior. The drug addict could be learning the lessons of Neptune with a depth it might take another person many lifetimes to learn.

Feelings of disillusionment are common under Neptune transits, and as depressing as this can be, it is often an important step in our development. When it is time for us to leave something behind, no matter how good it may have been for us formerly, we become disillusioned with it and find it no longer has much to offer. When an apple is ripe, it drops off the tree, and when it is time for a baby to be born, the conditions in the womb begin to deteriorate, triggering off the birth hormones in the baby's brain. Neptune in our natal charts has been likened to a womb. When it is time for us to leave whatever womb we've been en-

---

7. Don't ask me where it came from! I saw it on a plaque once.

trenched in as adults (a habit, a group, a situation), a Neptune transit creates disillusionment and dissolves our bonds to it. Thus disillusionment, however painful, is but a stage in our growth, signalling that we are ready to move on.

Another purpose of disillusionment under a Neptune transit is to loosen our ties with the material world and make us yearn for the spiritual side of life. Many of the things we become *dis*illusioned with were only *illusion* to begin with. Buddhism and other spiritual teachings reveal that all in this world is transitory and illusory (Maya), while the world beyond death is real and everlasting. During Neptune transits, many people have religious experiences that change their whole life. Psychic powers are often awakened that enable us to contact other planes of existence.

When you do finally awaken to the spiritual side of life, however, it may take many years to deal with it in a balanced way. The novice seeker is prone to false trails, self-delusion, and ideas that are quite bizarre. An important process, during Neptune transits, is to sort out, either by careful thought or bitter experience, what is of value and what is false among spiritual teachings. Neptune rules both psychic experience and fraud, so there are many phony or misguided occultists. Using psychic powers and finding our way among spiritual teachers is like learning to walk all over again, only more difficult. With all that fog, who can see where to put your feet?

CHAPTER 11

HOW TO DEAL WITH PLUTO — LET GO AND LET LIVE

Pluto has been called the planet of female sexuality by astrologer Charles Jayne and others. At first, I felt this was a rather sexist statement; but on deeper study, I find I agree. While both men and women give birth to things other than children, Pluto represents a female type of reproductive process in which you allow something new to grow within yourself out of the substance of yourself. Like the female sexual organs, this process is internal and hidden and, like pregnancy, it develops over a long period. A key word which has been assigned to Pluto is "transformation." The effect of Pluto is change and transformation; and whether its results are positive or negative depends on how well we are able to accept the changes it brings. I believe that Pluto's negative effects are related to a response which I will be calling *holding on* and the positive ones to a response I will be calling *letting go.*[1] We will be talking about "Plutonian" people a great deal in this chapter. Plutonians include people with planets in Scorpio, a number of planets in the eighth house, and those whose Pluto is near the Ascendant or Midheaven or aspecting the Sun or Moon.

Negative Expressions of Pluto

One negative expression of Pluto is the syndrome described by Charles Jayne of intensely emotional, possessive, jealous persons who bind others to themselves through guilt and over-protection. I recognize in this some of the dynamics of "controlling persons" who manipulate everyone around them and are afraid of every new situation because something may happen that they can't direct. They typically get their way through subtle ways of making others feel guilty. Although men can certainly display these types

---

1. Pluto has been a subject of special study for me due to its prominence in my chart. A number of people have contributed to my understanding of it, but I would especially like to acknowledge my friend and colleague Nancy Colin, who worked through with me a number of the insights in this chapter. The greater part of this chapter was published by Dell Horoscope Magazine, 6/75 issue, as "Transforming Pluto's Negative Influences," and is reprinted with their permission.

of behavior, women have had to rely more heavily on such mechanisms due to their lack of more direct means of power. This has been especially true in old-world or machismo-oriented cultures, where the wife was supposedly totally submissive to her husband.

Further negative Plutonian behavior has been described by other astrologers, notably Richard Ideman. There is the unrelenting vindictiveness of the scorpion type of Scorpio. (Remember that the scorpion destroys itself when it stings.) There can be a holding in of emotions that stifles spontaneity—a rigid control over anger in particular and a deep fear that any expression of anger will be violent. People who hold in anger this way are especially prone to engage in intense and violent love affairs or to provoke violence from others.

Another misuse of Pluto is secretiveness, self-protectiveness, and defensiveness that is so suspicious of others that it borders on paranoia at times. Because Plutonians are afraid to be open about their thoughts and feelings, even the rather normal human needs and feelings are hidden, so that these people come to believe they are abnormal and alien to the human race. This contributes a great deal to the aloneness most Plutonians struggle with constantly. An experience like a therapy or sensitivity or consciousness-raising group can do a great deal toward counteracting the feeling of being alien, because we come to see that many of our thoughts, reactions, and experiences are shared by others. Sharing, in fact, is a key lesson for Plutonians to learn, for in possessing a thing completely, you are alone.

The isolated, hermit-like existence of Plutonian people is often alternated with symbiotic relationships, smothering setups where neither partner can seem to exist or make a move without the other. Isolation and symbiosis are opposite ends of the same pole; and Plutonians may swing back and forth between the two extremes, never really comfortable with either, until they finally learn to operate somewhere in the middle. That same sense of isolation can often be a cause of promiscuity, which is seldom sexually satisfying and is often brought on by a great need to be close and escape the inner aloneness.

I can see that other emotional problems must be related to the holding-on/holding-in of Pluto. The obsessive-compulsive personality is one who hangs on and repeats an action or thought. Frigidity and impotency are the control or holding in of sexual feelings and the inability to let go in an orgasm. In modern relationships where the man is sensitive enough to want to satisfy the woman sexually, her orgasm can become the focus of a tremendous power struggle. This would appear to be the case also in the much-discussed "new impotency," a trend that men are blaming on Women's Liberation—an unconsciously with-holding response to women's growing demand for equality and fulfillment. In addition to these emotional difficulties, "holding in" also produces certain physical problems, such as those due to chronic muscular tensions. These, I would imagine, would include headaches, backaches, constipation, and arthritis. (Bioenergetic therapists are discovering and working with these chronic muscular tensions and their associated emotional derivations.)

Pluto & the Disease Cancer

Astrology relates Pluto to the disease cancer, and this would seem to be metaphysically correct. According to metaphysicians, the person who develops cancer is holding on to an old hurt, secret, or situation out of the past and is being literally eaten up with resentment. Even the popular press is beginning to recognize there is a connection between the emotions and cancer. Certain medical facilities and psychotherapists are providing psychological testing and psychotherapy as one of the tools for helping cancer patients. There have been some incredible results, even with terminally ill patients, when helped to find a new outlook on life which enables them to make some basic changes in themselves and their lifestyles.[2]

---

2. "Can Your Emotions Help You Resist Cancer?" Eda LeShan, *Women's Day*, 3/75, p. 64.

A research project done by Dr. Lawrence LeShan involved testing and interviewing 450 cancer patients and a control group of people who did not have cancer. He found that 72% of the cancer patients fit a particular personality pattern, while only 10% of the participants who didn't have cancer fit it. The article is worth quoting because it contains a very Plutonian emotional configuration:[3]

> . . . From early childhood on, these patients had had serious problems establishing warm and satisfying love relationships. They felt rejected and unloved and were constantly searching for ways to please others. Afraid of losing whatever acceptance they had, they almost never expressed their own intense feelings of anger, loneliness, hopelessness, and self-hatred. Although suffering severe psychic pain, they were considered by others to be unusually fine, thoughtful, sweet, gentle, and uncomplaining.
>
> Sometime during their adult lives, these people had been able to achieve a relationship with a person or with their work that brought their first experiences of joy and fulfillment. In some cases this was a successful marriage, in others the pleasures of parenthood or a career that seemed to bring our long-hidden talents and strengths. But in each case the patients discovered hidden reserves of energy and, for the first time in their lives, felt truly optimistic about themselves and the future.
>
> Then this phase of their lives ended. A marriage developed serious problems, or the much-loved spouse died; children grew up and left home; the individual was forced to retire from work that had been a central focus of life. After the loss these patients retreated into old patterns of behavior. They became isolated and experienced great fatigue. They felt rage and grief but never expressed their feelings openly. They seemed to accept their fate as their due—as if they had known all along that this would happen . . . Then, sometime within the next six months to eight years, they developed cancer.

As you can see, there are so many devastating effects of this holding-in response in Pluto that it is no wonder Pluto and Scorpio have such a bad name. Yet it is our use of the planet's energy rather than the planet itself that is bad. The power of the planet can be used for either good or bad; and we choose, consciously or unconsciously, how we will use it. With the greater awareness we can gain by studying astrology comes a greater responsibility to make

3. Op. cit., p. 99.

the best use of each planet and sign. This is nowhere more true than with Pluto, a planet with tremendous power for either destruction or transformation. Let us look, then, to see how Pluto can be used constructively to change our lives for the better.

The positive expressions of Pluto, which I have labeled *letting go*, are actually the allowing of change and transformation to happen—or even bringing them about. Rebirth and regeneration are words which describe this positive use of Pluto—like the phoenix side of Scorpio, rising out of its own ashes. In the article quoted above, for instance, a number of patients treated with psychotherapy did not die, but instead were reborn, because the treatment freed them from old patterns. Many began living a whole new life, making some amazing changes of career and life style. Both psychotherapy and cancer are related to Pluto, and in an almost homeopathic fashion, the positive Pluto energies were used to counteract the negative Pluto energies with a healing result. To be regenerated is to be renewed, rejuvenated, or healed. Thus, a tremendous healing ability can be developed in most Plutonians, whether through traditional medical channels or through spiritual healing or psychotherapy.

Other uses of Pluto can be quite dangerous because they have tremendous power for either good or harm. Hypnotism, for example, can be positive when used for healing or giving up habits, but negative when used to achieve control over others. Witchcraft, voodoo, and other arts our culture calls magic—because we do not understand their principles—also have power both for healing and for destruction or control. Mediumship, in which the control of the ego is relinquished to another, is a Plutonian activity but leaves the medium open to possession (according to Edgar Cayce) or to taking on the physical and mental conditions of those she or he is trying to help. The great power and danger of arts such as these are precisely why much occult knowledge was carefully guarded and not revealed to the public at large. (Occult and psychic powers actually are a combination of Neptune and Pluto.) It is significant, I feel, that Pluto itself was hidden from us until the 1930's and that since its discovery man has made tremendous strides in understanding both psychology and the occult, which are associated with it. It is as if we are now *ready* to or else *forced* to deal with the things Pluto rules.

My colleague, Nancy Colin, pointed out to me that the association of Pluto with still another twentieth-century phenomenon, nuclear power and atomic energy, is very appropriate. In a nuclear reaction, one kind of matter is transformed into another, and tremendous energy is released in the process. Pluto's transformations in our lives can be like this; and as in nuclear reactions, the released energy needs to be strictly channeled or it can run away with itself and create the havoc and destruction of a nuclear explosion. Psychological fallout, in the form of resentment, guilt, or regrets, can linger on for years. On the other hand, blocking Pluto—resisting the change or transformation—can create a backlash of destructiveness either turned in on the self, of which the ultimate form is suicide, or turned loose on others, of which the ultimate form is murder. On a political level, for example, the conservative efforts to block social change have created underground revolutionary activity.

Since we can see that Pluto cannot ultimately be held in or shut down, let's turn our attention now to some ways to transform our use of Pluto from a negative to a positive level. Many of these ideas are drawn from psychology, particularly modern humanistic psychology, and from the Science of Mind (also known as Religious Science or the New Thought Movement), because it seems to me that astrological insights must often be combined with another discipline, such as spiritual healing, for a full transformation of consciousness to occur.

My first understanding is that in order to lessen the negative, holding-on/in effects of Pluto, we must learn to accept—even embrace—change. If we are not willing to accept changes, they may be made for us, sometimes in destructive ways. Change and transformation are inevitable and even positive parts of life. If we want to continue to grow and progress, we must be willing for change to occur. When a living thing has stopped growing, it has already begun to die.

Certainly, Pluto's transformations may be painful at times. In coming through a Pluto transit of her own, Nancy Colin likened it to giving birth to yourself all over again without the anaesthetic. It seems to me, however, that, just as in labor pains, the more you tense up and resist this rebirth, the more painful it will be. Like natural childbirth, if you can welcome and work with the change, it will not be as painful. Even with the more difficult or destructive-seeming events that take place under Pluto, however, the final outcome can frequently be seen as positive.

Most forms of change are very hard for us to accept. Religious Science tries to counterbalance this reluctance by constantly telling us to let go of the past and live in the now. Their major technique of healing, a special kind of prayer called a treatment, is always done in the present tense. The desired condition, such as good health, is affirmed as existing or fulfilled right now. Past belief patterns (or relationships that hold the person back) are negated and dissolved, as are current conditions contrary to the goal. This focus on the now and the letting go of past negatives are necessary to the healing, and there have been some wonderful healings, even of cancer, with their treatments.

My second thought on how we can change the level of our Pluto is to gradually train ourselves to give up the negative Plutonian ways of relating to each other—ways like jealousy, possessiveness, guilt-binding, controlling, and manipulating. Besides holding us down in our growth and progress, responding on the lower level of Pluto invites further negative forms of Pluto, such as withdrawal, violence, or the physical consequences we have already spoken about.

Another Plutonian way of relating which we need to work hard at eliminating is vindictiveness, revenge, and resentment. Two people embroiled in this way are just as tied and entrapped as two people in a symbiotic "love" relationship—and very often that is how they started out. A frequent motive for murder is jealousy and revenge between lovers. Even when vengefulness does not go to the extreme of murder, it paralyzes the growth of both people and ties up energies that could better be used elsewhere. Religious Science and some occult teachers concur that this way of relating is dangerous; the destructiveness you let loose and set into motion always comes back to you magnified many times. Even if it does not go to that extent, you aren't free emotionally to attract a new love into your life until you've given up the old one.

How can we learn to give up relating to others in these negative ways? A primary way is self-awareness. The patterns may be so subtle and habitual (viewed as the only way of relating because we learned it at home) and so covered over with defenses that they can be terribly hard to see at first. They may be brought to light by careful watchfulness, possibly accompanied by some group therapy or encounter groups, where such behavior is often more readily played out and called to your attention than in individual therapy. Another corrective is for us to gradually accept and recognize that we are individuals and can never really bind or be bound to another person. Regardless of how many close and loving relationships we have, each person has his/her own tasks, talents, and interests and must be completely free to develop to the fullest in his/her own individual way and time sequence. All ties which prevent self-development are destructive. We can and must develop relationships with others based on a love that allows each one freedom and fuller self-expression.

The fear of our essential isolation is, I feel, fairly universal. Two things can help us to overcome it. One is to concentrate on your own development, learning to express to the fullest your own unique gifts and creative talents—

and we all have them—so that you feel complete and ful-filled instead of inadequate and inconsequential. When you love yourself more, you have less need for the unconditional love and acceptance of others and more inner serenity. The second thing to know is that while we are separate, we are really all one. Religious Science and other groups teach that there is one Power which created and which permeates every person, place, and thing in the universe. Therefore, while we alone are responsible for our own development, we are one with the Universe, which loves and assists us as part of itself.

Let us suppose that you are in a destructive Plutonian relationship. What can you do to change it or get free of it? If therapy hasn't wrought the desired change and you feel you must leave the relationship, then you must let go emotionally of that tie. Religious Science teaches us to think the following whenever that person comes to mind: "Bless _____ and release him to his higher good." At first, you may feel hypocritical blessing someone you would rather curse; but as you continue to do this, your feeling about that person will change and so will the relationship. Other spiritual teachers say to make a white cross in your mind over that person every time you think of him/her. Catharine Ponder has much to say about healing and chang-ing relationships in her beautiful book, *The Prospering Power of Love* (Unity, 1966).

Pluto's Relationship to Sex

Another important area of life which is related to the eighth house, Pluto, and Scorpio is sexuality. I have been trying to understand for a long time why so many religious teachings are down on sex, and I think I am beginning to see it. So often a sexual relationship between two people leads into other Plutonian ties in the relationship—to possessive-ness, jealousy, relating to others on the basis of lust only, to trying to control and manipulate, and to using sex compul-sively as an escape from isolation. It seems to me, however, that there must be a positive kind of sexuality that would transform, regenerate, and energize the person rather than bring the letdown that many feel when they find themselves just as isolated as before. After all, there is no birth without sex; and positive sexuality must be related to a new birth of creativity and growth. This can happen when we have begun to learn to use our Pluto energies positively and have gotten far enough away from the need to possess and control others. This can take place between healthy, creative individuals who are able to be free though related.

Pluto Transits

A major issue that can come up under a Pluto transit is that of control and the use of power. The Plutonian person primarily exerts control over the self, and all too often may be unable to express anger or other negative feelings outwardly, at quite a cost to their spontaneity and their mental and physical health. Under a Pluto transit, the suppressed feelings, even from the very distant past, may come out and be quite painful to deal with. Once this is done, however, you are much freer and rid of the great burden this kind of control can be. The other type of Plutonian control manifests in relationships, where a subtle power struggle may be going on, playing on guilt and dependency. Under a Pluto transit, you may become aware and want to change to a new way of relating. Sometimes this means relating to different people entirely, with a painful process of disengagement. In the end, however, you wind up with a freer and healthier set of relationships.

Almost any problem area in your chart and your life can be healed by a Pluto transit to that area. You often go through a purging process, whereby the problem is intensified to a critical point, then you withdraw and look inward at its causes, and then slowly try to deal with it. This is not easy, but you become a stronger and healthier person through the process. A Pluto transit to a key area of your chart (Sun, Moon, Ascendant for example) is bound to bring a type of rebirth.

Many astrologers feel that a transit of one outer planet (Saturn, Uranus, Neptune or Pluto) to another is not significant because these are not "personal" planets. I do not find this to be so. In particular, I have found the transit of Pluto over natal Neptune to be highly significant in the lives of my clients—especially those with Pluto or Neptune prominent in their natal charts. In many cases Neptune had earlier been operating on a negative level (confusion, irrationality, masochism, or escapism) and with the transit of Pluto over that area, it began to operate in a higher way. In many cases, including my own, this was the beginning of interest or study in the occult and spiritual realm. The house and sign matters of Neptune's location are deeply affected and usually healed.

Summary

In this chapter we have considered Pluto in many forms, both positive and negative, and have examined just a few ideas on how to change the level of expression from a negative to a positive one. As we are more and more able to let go rather than hold on in reacting to changes and transformations in our lives, our experience of Pluto will seem less destructive and more and more positive. In many ways, this process seems the death of our old earth-bound, egotistical selves. Evangelical Christians say, "Ye must be born again." I feel this contains a profound truth that has nothing to do with the church. We must be willing to let the old die in order to let something new be born into our lives.

PART THREE
SOME HELP WITH CHART INTERPRETATION

CHAPTER 12

THE NEGLECTED
NODES OF THE MOON

The Nodes of the Moon are greatly neglected by modern astrologers, possibly because there is much confusion and vagueness about their meaning. In this chapter, several ideas about the significance of the Nodes will be explored and evaluated to see how they can help individuals understand themselves better.[1]

Before examining the theories, we may want to clarify what the Nodes are astronomically. As the earth revolves around the Sun, it marks a plane called the ecliptic which cuts through the earth and stretches to infinity. The Moon cuts across the ecliptic in two places 180° apart during its monthly revolution around the earth. These two places are the North Node (☊ or Dragon's Head) and the South Node (☋ or Dragon's Tail). Only the North Node is shown in the ephemeris, but the South Node should be placed in the chart at the opposition point, 180° away. During the yearly revolution, the earth gradually shifts its axis, and the orbit of the Moon changes to accommodate to this. Thus the Nodes move backwards, retrograde, about 3' a day. The rate of motion is not constant, however, and since most ephemerides show a constant rate, they can be as much as 1½° in error. The new *American Ephemeris* by Neil Michelsen shows both the mean Node (one used by most ephemerides) and the true Node. Even without the exact position, however, we will usually be able to find the signs and houses occupied by the Nodes in a chart. These are the critical pieces of information in most interpretations. Let us turn, then, to some of the theories about the meaning of the Nodes.

Many of the ancient schools of thought, such as the Indian, viewed the Nodes as malefic or evil, harbingers of karmic events. The Indians saw the North Node as showing the nature of Mars, the South as showing the nature of

---

1. This chapter is reprinted from *Kosmos*, the journal of the International Society for Astrological Research, Vol. 3:5, Jan. '71.

Saturn. Whether or not there is something to this theory, it produces only fearful anticipation rather than a constructive direction toward which we can work. The Theosophists also view the Nodes as karmic. They feel that if someone's Sun is in conjunction with your Nodes, it is a fated karmic relationship, beyond your control. This again leaves you with no direction—is the relationship merely to be endured, or what can be done to work off the karma? What is the meaning of a planet other than the Sun contacting the Nodes?

Clara Darr considers this last question in her pamphlet on chart comparison called *Keys to Interrelations*. She goes through each planet and its meaning when conjunct the North or South Node of another person. For instance, she views Mercury conjunct the North Node of another as mental harmony, bringing publicity or beneficial contacts, and Mercury conjunct the South Node of another as bringing mental confusion to either person. Her view, once more, is that the North Node is beneficial while the South Node is adverse. In doing a horary chart, she sees the house position of the North Node as the area where you will receive extra assistance, the house of the South as where deceit will occur.[2]

R.C. Davison, in his paperback beginning text, *Astrology*, emphasizes more the meaning of having a planet in your own chart near the North Node as showing qualities to be developed, while planets near the South Node are overdeveloped and habitual in their expression. Further, he feels that all planets in the half circle from the North to the South Nodes are new qualities and faculties to be developed, while planets in the half circle from the South to the North Node are the working out of past patterns and tendencies. He considers the dispositors of both Nodes as further evidence.[3]

Reinhold Ebertin and other members of the cosmobiological school of astrology look at the North Node as one's

2. Clara Darr. Lecture on Horary Astrology, 4/22/70, New York.
3. Davison, Ronald C. *Astrology*, ARC Books, New York, 1963, pp. 142-3.

ability to adapt and unite with others, to form associations and alliances, to be sociable and obliging. The South Node shows where you lack adaptability, are unsociable, or where you may be involved in antisocial conduct. The Nodes are involved in their midpoint configurations and interpreted as associations with people in one's life.[4] Uranian astrologers use a similar meaning for the Nodes. They see them as the relationships you will make with people in life, and as significant in marking such major events as birth, marriage, and death by transits and progressions.

Marc Edmund Jones feels that the North Node represents your potential and the area where progress is made through effort—although progress flows easily there when the effort is made. Your greatest protection and support come to you at that point. He feels the North Node is also a measure of your character and determination. Jones sees the South Node as the point of self-undoing, representing the things we do not have to struggle for because they are inherent or come naturally. Our innate talent, genius, and charm is shown at the South Node, but it can also be our Achilles' heel, as it is the path of least resistance and can easily run away with us.[5] In another place, in *Essentials of Astrological Analysis*, Jones presents a provocative and perhaps more hopeful view of the South Node, even though he resorts to the old type of thinking of the South Node as the doer, rather than as a part of oneself symbolically represented. He says that the South Node encourages people to break away from themselves and from external reality in either very creative or very self-destructive ways. He feels that it is self-undoing when it dissipates or debases the real resources or promise of the person, not when it awakens the person to new and fresh potentials in everyday self-expression, at which times it is tremendously important in achievement and in regeneration of the personality. He concludes, "Thus the Moon's South Node indicates what

---

4. Ebertin, Reinhold. *The Combination of Stellar Influences*, 1969, pp. 54-55.
5. Marc E. Jones. *Fifteen Points in Professional Astrology*, Aquarian Agent, Vol. 1:7, p. 9 (1970).

perhaps may be the greatest inner strength or the most superficial weakness of every chart."[6] (In his theory, the South Node of the Moon sounds very much like Neptune.) Although I don't agree that the South Node, *per se*, causes anything, I do feel that there is merit in his theory if you regard the South Node as a part of you which can demonstrate the potentials he discusses.

Dane Rudhyar, in *The Astrology of Personality*, has a lengthy chapter on the Nodes of the Moon and those of other planets.[7] His ideas are very similiar to Jones' in many ways. Rudhyar views the Nodes as representing an axis between individuation (☊) and automatism (☋). He sees the North Node as signifying the future destiny of the individual—new accomplishments and faculties to be developed. The South Node looks back at past accomplishments, becoming negative simply because nothing new is developed as we take the path of least resistance. Rudhyar does not see the South Node as evil or destructive in itself, but only as we become a slave to the past, and fail to adjust to new conditions. As he says, "The past will have to die before the future can live." The faculties characterized by the North Node, he states, are those which life constantly forces us to develop, but we are also amply rewarded for efforts consciously made in that direction. Rudhyar also points out that the South Node's position may show when we can *release* creative "seeds" naturally and spontaneously. Rudhyar points out the usefulness of the Nodes in our quest for self-understanding and self-betterment. Studying the placements of the Nodes can help us detect where we are following the path of least resistance—usually carefully hidden from ourselves and others—and where we need to work consciously to develop ourselves.

In reflecting on what the Nodes may represent on a psychological level, my own idea is that the North Node

---

6. Marc E. Jones, *Essentials of Astrological Analysis,* Sabian Press, NYC, 1960, pp. 346-348, 359-361.

7. Rudhyar, Dane. Chapter 9, "Planetary Interweaving," *The Astrology of Personality,* Doubleday Paperback Edition, Garden City, N.Y., 1970, pp. 287-306.

may represent the ego-ideal—that configuration of characteristics which represents what we most want ourselves to be like. The South Node may represent the opposite—that group of characteristics within ourselves which we strongly reject, resist recognizing, and even project onto other people. A friend of mine has North Node in Virgo, South Node in Pisces, and a considerable amount of water in her chart. As a beginner, she was reading one of the Sun sign books and exclaimed, "Why couldn't I have been born a Virgo!" On the other hand, she strongly dislikes Pisces—"those Pisces" are sloppy, weak, emotional people with no backbone. This illustrates what I was just conjecturing about the Nodes. It seems to me that this theory would be fairly simple to test out by taking a survey among non-astrologers who are familiar with the Sun signs to see whether their prejudices for and against various signs correspond with the placement of their Nodes. Some preliminary testing among my friends and clients seems to support it.

Isabel Hickey devotes an entire chapter to the Moon's Nodes in her book, *Astrology, A Cosmic Science.*[8] Her ideas are basically the same as Jones' and Rudhyar's. What is helpful, however, is that she takes both the North and South Nodes through each sign and house to explore their meanings. As she points out, the Nodes are in each sign for about a year and a half, so that the significance of the signs they are in is fairly general, applying to everyone born in that year and a half. The house position, on the other hand, is very individual and specific because it is related to the date, time and place of birth. In reading Hickey's descriptions of the Nodes in the signs and houses it seems that *both* have meaning and need to be combined, along with the meaning of any planet near the Nodes or aspecting them. And, since we need to develop our own thinking power (☊) instead of relying on Hickey (☋), let us work on some examples to see how these various theories help in the interpretation of individual charts.

---

8. Hickey, Isabel. Chapter 21, "The Moon's Nodes," in *Astrology: A Cosmic Science*, Altieri Press, Brideport, Conn., 1970, pp. 198-203.

Two fashionable issues about the houses immediately confront us and may even be part of the reason the Nodes are neglected. The first issue is whether the houses, and, particularly, their rulerships, are valid at all. Since I derive a great deal of meaning from the placement of the Nodes in the houses, I tend to put aside this particular controversy. Somewhat more meaningful to me is the second issue, that of which house system to use. In cases where the Nodes are near the cusp of a house, a change of house system may change the house placement. In very close cases, the Node may well be acting on both houses and in some way combining them. The reader may wish to try different systems to see which one gives the most appropriate and consistent meaning for the Node's placement. A third problem with regard to houses is that our understanding of their meanings needs to be broadened. Often we think of each house only in terms of a few keywords. A blatant example is the second house, which we equate with money. There are many more possible meanings for the second house, as we will see in our examples.

In broadening our concepts of the houses, it is often helpful to think of the sign and planet linked to it in the natural zodiac. For the second house, this is the sign Taurus and the planet **Venus**. The question is, where do we stop with this? Is the second house totally identified with Venus and Taurus, or is it more limited than that (and where are the limits), or does it have specific meanings not related to either Venus or Taurus? Much thought, observation, and research is needed to find some of these answers. The Ebertins seem to consider the houses and the signs interchangeable, since their descriptions of the Nodes in the houses and signs are combined, just as for all the planets.[9]

Since we would like to understand the second house better, let us see what it might mean for someone to have the North Node in Virgo in the second house, South Node in

9. Ebertin, Reinhold. *The Combination of Stellar Influences*, Germany, 1969, pp. 44-45.

Pisces in the eighth. To start with the traditional and obvious significance of the second and eighth houses, this means developing your own personal resources—financial, emotional, and spiritual—rather than relying on other people's resources. This is quite profound and important, but what additional meanings can we find? If we think of the second house as Taurus and the eighth as Scorpio, other meanings come to us. There can be the need to develop sensuality as opposed to sexuality; conservation and constructiveness rather than tearing down people, things and ideas; devotion rather than domination; acceptance rather than destructive criticism; peace of mind and placidity rather than emotional intensity; the practical, concrete and everyday rather than the occult and arcane. These are obviously some of the more negative manifestations of Scorpio and more positive manifestations of Taurus, but this type of emphasis seems to reflect the meaning of the Nodes. North Node in the eighth or Scorpio would work toward development of the more positive aspects of Scorpio.

If we think of the second house as Venus and the eighth as Pluto, other meanings suggest themselves. There could be the need to accept and love rather than to probe and delve; to join with others rather than to isolate the self; to relate with friendship and love rather than with bonds of psychological dependency and guilt; to be straight-forward and open rather than secretive and devious; to trust rather than to doubt and suspect the other. Not all of the ideas we have just generated about the North Node in the second and South Node in the eighth may be valid, but they need to be tried. The technique, however, seems valid and can be used with all other combinations of Nodes in houses and signs to generate new ideas and broaden our concepts.

What additional information can we get about this same person from the Nodes being in Virgo and Pisces? Virgo, where the North Node is, can be related to work, service, discrimination, analytical thinking, and to some extent to sexual fidelity. The South Node in Pisces could mean idealism, escapism, dreaminess, and over-emotionality. To enlarge upon the earlier technique, this is almost like comparing Mercury to Neptune. Adding this to what we considered about the second house-eighth house placement, we get a picture of someone whose task in life is to build something concrete, tangible, and practical, rather than losing himself in an other-worldly, dreamy, escapist life. This person has to be self-sufficient and work to support himself rather than living from the financial and emotional resources of other people. Further, he has to learn to relate to others in an open and straight-forward way, to be the servant rather than to gain domination through psychological bondage or sexuality. He must learn to be constructive, practical, and logical, rather than destructive and overly emotional. These are just a few of the ideas that could come from this combination of the sign and house placement of the Nodes.

What if, to further complicate the interpretation, the person has a planet conjunct one of these Nodes? Mars conjunct the North Node in Virgo in the second might aid by giving energy and zest toward developing the necessary characteristics—or might hinder because of its hypercritical propensities. However, the whole chart would have to be considered to see what Mars specifically represents in a particular chart. The whole chart would have to be considered, in any event, to see what in the chart helps or hinders the tasks represented by the Nodes. Suppose this same person with the North Node in Virgo in the second (South Node in Pisces in the eighth) also had Pluto in Cancer rising and Saturn in Taurus on the Midheaven. Pluto and Cancer rising would intensify the watery, eighth-house Scorpio and the Pisces qualities, and thus the personality projected to others (ascendant) would attract the very things that were already overdeveloped (♈). On the other hand, the strongly-placed Saturn would give stability, seriousness, and responsibility to work on the task represented by the North Node.

The Nodes appear to be important in charts other than the birth chart, particularly in the solar return. Through the years, the Nodes will pass through all the signs in the solar returns, just as we need to develop all twelve signs within us to be well-rounded. The house positions of the Nodes seem to be especially important in the solar return. A friend of mine, who had worked very hard to build a successful telephone answering service, was about to sell her business to be able to spend more time studying the occult. Her solar return showed the South Node conjunct the Sun in Virgo in the third house of communication and everyday intelligence, while the North Node was in Pisces in the ninth house of the higher mind. Another friend, a Sun-rising double Scorpio, was struggling consciously to conquer his domineering approach to people. His solar return showed the South Node in the tenth house of status, conjunct the kingly, super-Leo, fixed star Regulus. Over and over, the Nodes seem to have strong, unmistakable messages in the solar return. By watching their positions in these birthday charts every year, we can get fresh insights into our progress.

As we have seen, there are many factors to be considered in interpreting the Moon's Nodes in a chart. There are many insights to be gained, on various levels, by studying the Nodes. Much growth can occur from understanding what they represent, and the time spent studying and thinking about them can result in a clearer, surer way to progress.

CHAPTER 13

THE HOUSES OF THE HOROSCOPE: HOW INNER ATTITUDES DETERMINE OUTER REALITIES

Just as we saw earlier that we can't blame the planets and signs for what happens in our lives, neither can we blame the houses for the conditions that surround us. Again, they must be seen as describing rather than causing these conditions. Many astrology books contain superficial definitions of the houses of the horoscope; for instance, that the second house shows how you will fare in money matters, the fifth your children, the seventh your marriage partner, and so on. The descriptions sound like everything is determined by something outside yourself—by Fate, people in authority, the economy, or heredity. If you have Jupiter in the second, they would say, then luck will just keep coming your way in money matters.

My own belief—from studying psychology, metaphysics, and some of the deeper spiritual teachings—is that this kind of definition is backwards. Rather than external things determining your experiences, it is your inner attitudes, beliefs, emotions, and needs which act as magnets to determine the outer, tangible circumstances of your life. We must look at the houses to see what part we are playing in our own misfortunes and what responsibility we have in making our lives better. The houses show what we are attracting to ourselves by our subconscious attitudes. The person with Jupiter in the second house, for example, isn't lucky due to Fate, but to his own attitudes of openness, enthusiasm, and optimism that lead him to act on opportunities others might let pass by. In most cases, we make our own luck, good or bad. In this section we will go through each of the houses of the horoscope to see how inner attitudes toward the subject associated with that house can influence our experiences in that area. In any given chart, we can uncover those attitudes,

*Original version published in Dell Horoscope, 11/74, as "The Truth About the Houses—Inner Attitudes Determine Outer Realities." ©1974 by Dell Publishing Co., Inc. Reprinted with their permission.

many of which are unconscious, by thinking about the sign on the cusp of that house, any planets in the house, and the condition of the ruler of the house.

The First House

The first house is how others see us, which is determined by our outward behavior and the "vibes" we put out. The sign on the ascendant and the planets in the first show our way of trying to get along and get what we need from others. It is important that we analyze the first house to see how we come across. Its harmony or disharmony with needs and traits shown in the rest of the chart is crucial to our well-being. Consider the plight, for example, of a Leo native with Capricorn on the ascendant. Fun-loving Leo wants warmth and attention; but the Capricorn ascendant makes him come across as rather forbidding—self-sufficient, taciturn, and even gloomy, drawing out a different kind of response than the hungry lion needs. Look at your own first house from this point of view. Is what you are putting out going to get you what you need from others? If not, you must consciously try to express those needs and change your way of relating in order to get them met. Often it is hard for us to see exactly how we come across. The most ideal way is a video-tape of yourself, but since few of us have one available, you may need to rely on others to reflect it back to you. A sensitivity group or candid discussions with insightful friends may help you see yourself better. Even such things as an unposed photo or suddenly seeing yourself reflected in a mirror or a shop window can give you clues.

First-house behavior is generally learned very early, as ways of acting that your parents insisted on or that you had to adopt in order to get what you needed from them. Such patterns are often carried on long after they cease to be appropriate or helpful to us, such as the forty-year-old woman still playing the cute, coy child. Ask yourself where the behavior came from, whether it is adaptive in your current situation, and whether it is helpful to you in relating to others on an adult level. (Not all such behavior is bad; some of it can serve you quite well and makes up your own particular brand of charm.) First-house behavior is terribly important to understand because it is the first impression you make on people, and generally this is what stays with them. People usually take you at your own evaluation. If you come across as a nothing, that is how they will see you also. Thus, your own behavior determines a great deal of how people respond to you; and it is better to be conscious of that behavior and modify it, if necessary, to portray your real self and your real needs.

The Second House

The second house was mentioned briefly in the introduction to this chapter. We saw that it is traditionally seen as your money but that inner attitudes have a great deal to do with your external financial situation, as in the example of Jupiter in the second. Our culture has mixed and conflicting attitudes about money, and many young people are swinging back almost to the puritanical belief that it is the root of all evil. Yet money itself is neutral—only the way people handle it is good or bad. No doubt, dealing with money and possessions in a sound, well-balanced way is an important spiritual lesson we must master. Many of Jesus' stories had to do with money, notably the parable of the talents, where the servant who greatly increased what he was given was handsomely rewarded by his master. As in other areas of life, your attitudes determine your experiences in second-house matters. If you hate money or subconsciously feel it is evil, you are unlikely to have much of it or hold on to it when you do get it. The person with Pisces on the second or Neptune in the second, for instance, who is doubtlessly other-worldly, may feel it is not spiritual to have material things and feels that "God will provide." Consequently, his financial affairs are vague and confused, he never knows where his money goes, and he may suffer a good deal in financial matters until his attitudes are more balanced. Your attitudes toward both money and possessions are described by the second house in your chart.

Even more basic than the second-house relationship to finances is another meaning, your sense of values. What you value is a key thing to understand because it often becomes a focus of action in your life and leads to the formation of goals. The person with Sagittarius or Jupiter in the second values higher education, and this is another reason such people are "lucky" with money—the more you know and the better educated you are, even self-educated, the more you are likely to earn.

The Third House

We hear a lot these days about the importance of communication—between lovers, parent and child, employer and employee, and between groups in society. If you feel others don't understand you, look to the third house to see how well you make yourself understood. This house shows both your attitude and your approach toward this vital skill. Sagittarius on the third might be very open and invite communication from others, while Scorpio on the third can be quite reserved and can discourage communication by its biting and often sarcastic mode of speech. Each of these behaviors may reinforce itself—the Scorpio speech pattern can drive others away; then the person feels bitter and alone and thus communicates even less. The person with Sagittarius on the third, by contrast, has positive and interesting experiences with communication because they are open and wish to learn, so the desire to communicate keeps growing. On the other hand, the person with Sagittarius on the third might be dogmatic and resistant to others' ideas, while the person with Scorpio on the third might excel as a counselor through the ability to listen intensely and communicate on deeper levels. Since most people will manifest both the positive and negative sides of any sign, finding out the potential problems and expressing the sign on that cusp in a positive way can help your relationships with others immensely.

The third house also governs everyday mental activities and chores—not how well you grasp Sartre and Camus (that's the ninth house), but how well you balance your checkbook. It shows how you approach such matters, whether you are efficient at them, and how they affect you. The person with Neptune in the third, for example, may not know where they parked the car last night, but don't get so annoyed at them that you miss hearing the marvelous new spiritual insight they came up with this morning in the shower.

Brothers and sisters are traditionally associated with the third house, but it is more correct to say that the third shows not the actual people involved but how they affected you or how you experienced them. You may have Scorpio on the third and so were jealous of your brother, but another sibling who loved him might have Libra on the third. An only child who yearned for a brother or sister and even created an imaginary one might have Pisces on the third. Again, it is not the concrete, outer reality that is important but the inner reality, your feelings and attitudes about that situation.

The Fourth House

To the fourth house traditionally is ascribed such things as your home, your mother, your base of security, and heredity or parental influence. The basic needs or issues of the fourth house, as I see it, are nurturing and security. Nurturing (i.e., meeting the child's physical and emotional needs) is not limited to the mother, and can be provided by both parents or any number of people, but the sum experience of nurturing develops the infant's sense of what Erikson calls "basic trust." Whether the person is basically secure or insecure depends on how that nurturing was experienced. The fourth house, planets in it, and its ruler can describe for you what that experience was and what the person does to feel secure. The basic lesson to be learned, of course, is that security is to be found within ourselves, not in anything external. For example, the person with Taurus on the fourth had a rather calm, down-to-earth upbringing but may seek security in material possessions. The person with Aquarius on the fourth doubtlessly had an erratic childhood and may find security is not having a permanent home, being free to move around as he wishes.

As we were nurtured, so do we nurture; therefore, the fourth can also give clues to your behavior in a role where this is required of you, as in parenthood. The person with Taurus on the fourth may have had a more stable parental role model than the person with Aquarius on the fourth and so is able to provide more stability and security to their own offspring. However, on the negative side this is not a parent with a great deal of flexibility to meet our rapidly changing standards and conditions. They will be conservative when it comes to child-rearing. Also, who is to say that the person with Aquarius on the fourth has not had a better preparation to make the best of the Aquarian Age?

The Fifth House

Nowhere is the stultifying effect of traditional thought more apparent than in the interpretation of the fifth house, which has been assigned to represent your children. It is taken for granted that you will have them. Since a whole house of your horoscope is given over to them, it follows that they are seen as part of you and as extensions of yourself, rather than either of you being seen as separate individuals. Psychotherapists have seen the damaging effects of this kind of thinking. What about the person who is childless either by circumstance or choice? Is that house considered inactive or nonexistent? I have even heard the absurdly sexist statement that the fifth house in a woman's chart represents her children, while in a man's chart it represents his creative efforts. This presupposes two totally unproven ideas: one, that a man cannot make children his major concern; two, that women are less creative than men. There is no evidence whatsoever that women, if freed from the responsibilities of housework and child care, can not be every bit as creative as men. In fact, male "experts" are telling us that women are "right-brain dominated"—and the characteristics of right-brain dominated persons are exactly those attributed to artists and other creative people. They are sensitive, intuitive, and emotional; so women might be even more creative than men, given the chance.

It is more accurate to say that the fifth house shows your attitude toward children. Hopefully, as society becomes more enlightened, it will be your attitude rather than social pressure which will determine whether or not you have children. It is true that your fifth describes your children; but is is also true that your feelings and attitudes about children determine your child-rearing practices and, thus, play a great part in molding your offspring. Possibly more important, the fifth house shows your attitude toward the child within yourself, which then affects your ability to engage in other important fifth-house concerns—recreation and creative self-expression. If you are able, as few are, to be truly childlike, then you are able to release and renew yourself fully in play and are more likely to be creative. Most children are creative, but it is stifled and socialized out of them as they grow.

The fifth house describes both the areas in which you can be most creative and the ways your creativity can be brought out. For instance, the person with Scorpio on the fifth could well have something creative to offer in the realms of psychology and psychotherapy; and this would best be brought out when the person has the opportunity to be alone and think deeply and introspectively. The person with Gemini on the fifth, on the other hand, might release their creativity more easily in talking with others. Try analyzing your fifth house this way. Don't limit your concept of creativity to the traditional fine arts. A person with Mars in Cancer in the fifth might design and build a storage module for the closet that would be just as creative and certainly more practical than a painting or a poem. For another example, a Taurus on the fifth type of creativity might be landscaping.

Understanding your fifth house can help you release your creativity. This would include the sign on the fifth house, any planets in it, and the sign and house placement of the ruler of the fifth. You might also want to look at the sign and house placement of the Sun, which is the natural ruler of the fifth. Rod Chase has found that some of the most famous works of creative people reflect their Sun sign —e.g., Whistler, who is a Cancer, is famous for the painting of his mother. If you have Saturn in the fifth, don't persuade yourself that you aren't creative, because we all have a fifth house and we all have our own individual brand of creativity. To return to our original premise that inner attitudes determine outer realities, your creative block may be due to inner fears and inhibitions—perhaps the belief that you must be perfect or else not even try. Or perhaps an authority figure from the past taught you that it was frivolous to waste time on such pursuits. You best creative work would be of a Saturnian nature and might be in something like pottery or sculpture. Or, perhaps it means you will be more creative as you grow older. I don't know if Grandma Moses' birth time was ever found, but I'd be willing to bet she had Saturn or Capricorn connected with her fifth house in some way.

The Sixth House

Work and health are the twin concerns of the sixth house, and the two are inter-related on a very deep level. How many cases have you heard of where a person retired and then lost his health? Productivity and a feeling of usefulness can keep us feeling alive, alert, and healthy. For a person whose sixth house is emphasized, unhappiness in the work often shows up in poor health, and when work conditions change for the better, the health improves, too. Our attitudes toward work and our day-to-day job functioning are also shown by the sixth.

My basic premise in this chapter is that inner states and attitudes produce outer experiences, and this is particularly true when it comes to your health. Psychology and psychosomatic medicine are coming closer all the time to accepting the basic principle of metaphysics (especially that of Christian Science and Religious Science)—i.e., that the mind governs our physical health. Most physical problems have an emotional basis and express a conflict or tension within the person. Practitioners of Medical Astrology go wrong when they focus only on the physical side of illnesses shown in the sixth. Not only do they risk bringing on that very illness by the power of suggestion, but also they ignore the opportunity for avoiding or alleviating the illness through deciphering and resolving the underlying conflicts—those shown both in the sixth and in other parts of the chart.

Let's look at an example to make these points clearer. Take a person who has Uranus in the sixth, suggesting the possibility of an impediment in the circulation. Underlying this is restlessness and nervous tension brought on by the person's belief that he is restricted or not free in his work and daily living—in many cases, a false or defensive belief anyway, arising from the "shoulds" and "shouldn'ts" we were taught as children or the ambitions our parents had for us. By getting work where he is free to move around—or, better, by getting at the reasons he can't tolerate restriction by authority—the psychosomatic circulatory problem can be relieved or avoided altogether. Evidence to back up this work-health connection comes from the statistics on hypertension among black people, a Uranus-in-the-sixth kind of illness. They have always had less freedom of choice about their work than whites, and if this is improving it is only doing so very slowly. In all age groups, black people have more high blood pressure than whites, but it is most striking in the years 55-64, where hypertension affects 48.3% of black men, 36.3% of white men, 35.8% of black women, and 29.3% of white women.*

---

*Statistics taken from the *Hypertension Handbook*, by Merck, Sharp, and Dohme, 1974.

The Seventh House

To the seventh house belongs that all-important area of close, intimate relationships such as marriage. "Surely," you are thinking, "this is where your theory goes wrong. It is up to the other person whether he loves me and wants to be close to me." That is indisputable; yet we seem to single out people to fit into our unconscious needs, healthy or unhealthy. Some people are married over and over but always to someone who turns out to fit one basic pattern, no matter how dissimilar they seem on the surface. A woman with an alcoholic father often has one relationship after another with men she discovers "too late" are alcoholics. Even within the realm of dating, single people can find patterns in the people they date—especially those who they felt treated them badly.

If you despair of ever finding a happy relationship, such a pattern may be operating. Only when the unconscious needs are identified and dealt with can you hope for a different kind of relationship. Look at the sign on the seventh house, planets within it, and the condition of its ruler to see what patterns and needs within yourself your intimate relationships may be expressing. For instance, a person with Mars and Uranus conjunct in the seventh may repeatedly get involved with kinky and unstable partners. This person needs to express more of their own kinky and unconventional nature for themselves and to give themselves more freedom. They would then have less need to choose partners who would act it out for them.

My great astrology teacher, Richard Ideman, points out that another cause of seventh-house problems can relate back to what was said about the discrepancies between the first house and the needs shown in the rest of the chart. The seventh house is opposite the first; thus, we attract the opposite of what we put out. That is, your way of coming across (first house) "turns on" some people and "turns off" others; and the first-seventh axis can show you what is happening. Let's take a few examples. Capricorn rising has Cancer on the seventh. A person with Capricorn rising must always act strong and adequate and so might attract someone with unmet dependency needs— a Cancer or Cancerian type. Pisces rising has Virgo on the seventh. If you have Pisces rising you might act vague, confused, disorganized and helpless; so you would attract a Virgo or Virgo-type person who would relish the idea of making you over and bringing order into your life. As I pointed out before, your rising sign or ascendant may not be the real you at all, but merely the tactics you adopted as a child to get along. Thus, when you attract people on the basis of first-house behavior, you may be drawing to you those who do not meet your basic needs at all, so you are unhappy.

To return to our example, let's suppose that you have Capricorn rising and are also a Pisces native with strong dependency needs of your own. Through the Capricorn ascendant, you attract dependent people who can't take care of themselves and then feel unhappy because you want to be taken care of yourself at times. Only as you realize that your Capricorn front of never needing help is turning away those who might otherwise be glad to aid you can you begin to show some of your real needs and have them met. The first-seventh axis in our charts deserves a lot of thought, as it can help us understand many of the problems we have in relating to people from the most casual to the most intimate level.

The Eighth House

The eighth house has a number of seemingly unrelated meanings which we will find integrally related if we look deeply enough. For one thing, it has to do with the finances, resources, and values of other people. Its opposition to the second house—our own resources, finances, values—shows the need to achieve a balance between what is yours and what belongs to others, keeping them separate but equal and working on give and take in our dealings with others.

The eighth also has to do with birth and death, but these are not part of our day-to-day existence as others of the meanings are. The key eighth-house functions are sex and regeneration; and the new frontier of psychological knowledge seems to confirm that they belong together. Therapists and theorists, particularly of the bioenergetic school, are finding that consistently reaching orgasm releases the blocked-up energy flow, thus regenerating you physically and mentally.

It would seem that a thorough analysis of your eighth house is in order as a key to understanding your own sexual nature. Your difficulties, your attitudes toward sex, and those conditions that turn you on can be seen through the eighth house. This is another area where astrology can help you find your true selfhood, as apart from the strictures imposed on us by our society and its shoulds and shouldn'ts. If you have Aquarius on the eighth (an unexpected facet of the Cancer rising personality), then what turns you on will not be traditional and "respectable" but something modern and unusual—perhaps even group sex. The fact that society as a whole hasn't caught up with you shouldn't keep you from being fully expressed sexually. However, disapproval may wound that Cancer rising sensitivity and sometimes results in an Aquarian detachment from eighth house matters such as sex. It is important to know that it is society's hang-up rather than your own that results in this disapproval.

There are, of course, ways of regenerating yourself in addition to sex. People don't take the need for regeneration seriously enough, and that's why so many today walk around chronically fatigued. You probably have to work at regeneration just as seriously as you have to work at communication or marriage or any of the other areas of life. Richard Ideman points out that the eighth house is quincunx (150°) the first, so what regenerates you is something quite different from your day-to-day activities. The eighth house in your chart can teach you ways to regenerate yourself, and you can then turn to them more consciously and purposefully. The person with Pisces on the eighth, for instance, might find going to the movies or the seashore quite helpful. The person with Aries on the eighth might be renewed by physical labor on a project, like building something. The person with Taurus on the eighth might find it refreshing to garden or raise house-plants. Plan your next vacation around your eighth house and you may get much more out of it than usual.

The eighth house is the house of death and rebirth, and here again attitude is crucial. Every apparent death is a rebirth, whether it be the death of a person, a phase in your life, or your own death. If you fully trust that death is only an illusion, that no door closes without another one opening, then death will be a different kind of experience for you than for the person who does not have this kind of trust. If you have the sign Cancer on the eighth, for example, you may try to hang on too tightly to that person, to that phase of your life, or to life itself and thus prevent the rebirth or unnecessarily delay it.

The Ninth House

The ninth house, which is related to Jupiter, concerns the search for wisdom and knowledge. It is said to rule higher education, but this process can't be limited to the college years or to those with a college degree. I know self-educated people who are wiser and deeper than others with a doctorate. It also shows how you approach the workings of the higher mind—theory, abstract ideas, and philosophical questions. To try some examples, the person with Scorpio on the ninth has a powerfully analytical mind, capable of going deeply into abstract ideas. The person with Gemini on the ninth, by way of contrast, might approach it in a lighthearted and possibly superficial way (unless there are planets in the house to modify this). They would be quick to grasp ideas but just as quick to discard them for all the shiny new ones as they come off the press. On the other hand, the Scorpio on the ninth person might be terribly dogmatic and have difficulty communicating their thoughts, while the Gemini on the ninth person communicates well and would be an enjoyable teacher. Neither of these is better than the other. There is room in this world for all kinds of thinkers, because each has his own particular role to play in raising the level of consciousness of the human race.

The ninth house also represents your lifelong struggle to find out what you believe about the world, God, man, and life—roughly, your philosophy of life and your faith or religion. We all need something to believe in, and the ninth house in your chart shows what it is. Astrologer Jesse Hyllman says that the ninth shows the area in your life where you will find spiritual fulfillment. People with Taurus on the ninth, for instance, might find it in nature and in working with the land—this is what brings them close to God. Their philosophy would be a practical and even conservative one. Those with Pisces on the ninth or Neptune in it may find God in sitting by the ocean or listening to elevating music. These persons would be very mystical and emotional in their religion. They might have trouble in knowing what to believe because they could alternately be fooled by false teachings and then disillusioned, until they learn to open up their own inner ear to God, where they would find out what is the truth for them on their own personal path.

Your philosophy of life is much more than an abstract thing. It can guide your approach to life, to situations, and to other people. (It is related to the first house by a trine in the natural chart.) It probably even determines the way you vote. You may find it helpful to examine your ninth house in order to conceptualize and verbalize your philosophy of life, which may not have been conscious before. What is your outlook on life and how is it influencing the way you live? If inner beliefs determine outer realities, which has been our premise all along, then the ninth house has a great influence on all the rest of the houses and on your entire life experience.

The Tenth House

The tenth house is connected with your reactions to authority in all its forms—not just your parents' authority, but all people in authority over you. In psychoanalytic thinking, the latter grows out of the former. Several persons, who are under the same boss, would experience him/her in different ways, depending on how experiences with their parents conditioned them to perceive the boss's behavior. They could conceivably have three different Midheavens, or, since the Midheaven describes the career, similiar Midheavens with different aspects to it or different planets in the tenth house. The point is that our *perception* of the authority figure is as important as the kind of person the boss may actually be. If we unconsciously expect the boss to be punitive, we will behave in ways that ultimately cause the boss to have to be punitive—a situation that can persist over endless job changes.

The relationships between your attitudes toward authority and your potential for success are also quite profound. If you are either too rebellious or too timid and compliant, your chances for success are a lot less than someone who can deal with authority figures in a reasonable, responsible and balanced way. Furthermore, your attitude toward authority carries with it your attitude toward becoming an authority figure yourself. If you are uncomfortable with your own authority, you may not move very far along the road to success until you resolve that discomfort. Many people hit a snag in their career at the point where they have to assume a position of authority over others. And, yet, how many high positions are there today where you do not assume a managerial or supervisory role or have some employees under you?

The tenth house also shows how you would function in an authority position, and here is a logical connection

---

*Material about the tenth house was taken from my article, "Ten Things You Should Know About the Tenth House," *Astrology Today*, September 1976. © 1976 by CBS Publications, the Consumer Publishing Division of CBS, Inc.; reprinted with their permission.

with the original authorities, your parents. We live what we learn, and this makes it hard for us to be a different kind of authority figure than we experienced as children. This is because we consciously or unconsciously use our parents as role models, including how to raise our children and how to behave when we are in a position of authority. Most of us assume a position of authority at some times in our lives, even if it is "only" the role of parent . . . and the role of parent is probably the single most authoritative role possible, in view of the actual power involved and the omnipotence our children unconsciously invest us with.

With the trend toward alternate life styles and disenchantment with materialism, there are a growing number of people who can't relate to the idea of a career at all. Perhaps we will have to come to a deeper understanding of the tenth house . . . perhaps as what the person is trying to build or achieve and the ultimate impact of a person's life. Some people with Pisces on the tenth or Neptune in it, for example, may not appear to be a success in worldly terms because their goals may be other-worldly and mainly spiritual in nature. Maybe a study of the tenth house, the Midheaven, and all the aspects to it can give each of us a clue to that painful old question, "What is the ultimate meaning of my life?"

The Eleventh House

The eleventh house, related to Aquarius, deals with a number of things; but I wish to focus here on its relationship to friendship and to groups. Both can be helpful to us or can hold us back, so it is important that we integrate them well into the rest of our lives. (I owe many of the insights about this house to one of my truest friends, Rod Chase.) For the teenager, friendship and the peer group can take over and rule the life, seeming more important than any future goals or consequences. Many lives have been ruined by getting in with the wrong crowd. On the other hand, groups of friends have served as boosters and inspirations to creative people like Picasso and Gertrude Stein, to the Bauhaus people, and to the Impressionists, among others. Rightly used, friendship can be a great source of strength; but wrongly used, it can be quite destructive.

Good friends are a rare gift and can encourage and inspire us. All too often, however, the opposite is true: people you thought were your friends do not seem happy or are even actively jealous when you succeed or do something creative. Friendship is based on equality, but the false friend just wants to hold you down to his level. Many peer groups don't want you to be an individual either and will exert all kinds of subtle and blatant group pressure on you to conform to their ways, no matter how stultifying or nonproductive they are. The eleventh is opposite the fifth, and the opposition always indicates the need to achieve balance between two poles. The lesson of the eleventh is to learn to keep a happy medium between the human need for friendship and affiliation (eleventh) and the need for self-development and creative self-expression (tasks of the fifth and the Sun, which is behind it).

Group membership is similar to friendship in its positive and negative potential. Groups like Alcoholics Anonymous and Weight Watchers stand behind the person and help him develop—again the eleventh encouraging the fifth. But too many people use group membership to run away from themselves and stifle creative development—the eleventh pulling away from the fifth. Some people take up all their time as officers and committee members and going to endless meetings where nothing happens but talk. Our affiliations and friendships can waste much of our time and dissipate our creative energies unless we learn to make a positive selection of friends who encourage us and who are seeking to develop in ways that we also need.

The sign on the eleventh, planets within it, and position of its ruler are clues to understanding your needs and difficulties in the areas of groups and friendships, as well as to seeing what strengths and help they can supply you with. Often people will lose from friendship unless they learn to use those signs and planets connected with the eleventh in a positive way. The person with Saturn in the eleventh, for instance, may feel sad, lonely, and hopeless of ever having good friends as long as she is chasing after the local jet set, but will gain strength and wisdom when she looks for companions among more serious people, often those older than herself. In contrast to the time when her efforts were misplaced, she may even find herself quite popular. For another example, the person with Pluto in the eleventh might wind up a loner because "you can't trust anybody to get close to you." If you have read the earlier chapter on Pluto, however, you can speculate on some of the reasons for such a person's "bad experiences." Perhaps they are too possessive or play subtle power games with their friends, or they go at people too intensely with the idea of making them over. There are few real victims —you need to always look carefully at the ways people have contributed to or even subconsciously arranged patterns of unhappy experiences.

The Twelfth House

Each of the houses contains endless wisdom and insight, and one chapter—or even a book—could not begin to explore all of it. This is nowhere more true than with the misunderstood and much-maligned twelfth house, the so-called house of secrets and sorrows. In order to focus, we will concentrate here on the twelfth house concerns of repression and self-undoing, for what we keep secret from ourselves can cause us the most sorrow.

Repression is a psychological defense mechanism whereby unpleasant and unacceptable thoughts, experiences, needs, fears, and wishes are forced out of the conscious and into the unconscious. Sometimes, due to the nature of the wish, this is done so quickly and so habitually that we are not consciously aware of it. The repressed feelings do not go away; they continue to rumble around in the unconscious and ferment trouble. Neuroses and neurotic behavior of various kinds generally derive from repressed material. Repression is connected with the twelfth house. The sign on the twelfth and any planets in it can show us what kinds of emotions, needs, and past events we are repressing. You might even go so far as to say that the twelfth can show you the wellspring of your neurotic behavior. The twelfth has its good and positive aspects, too; but the more energy you divert into repression, the less energy is available for the positive expression of twelfth house powers. Uncovering, examining, and dissolving your bondage to the secrets and sorrows of the past can free you to develop the twelfth's spiritual side.

Let's look at one example of how the twelfth house energy can be diverted from self-destructive to constructive use. A person of my acquaintance with Leo rising and the Sun in Leo in the twelfth is in a real double bind when it comes to ego. The Sun in Leo, Leo rising, and the ruler of the Ascendant (i.e., the Sun) in Leo all point to a person who wants to be the center of attention at all times. Yet this crucial Leo Sun is in the twelfth house, so we get a picture that somehow the person was taught that it is not good to want so much attention. How, then, will the hungry Lion get fed? In the person's tempestuous twenties, it was via self-destructive ways of getting attention—psychosomatic illnesses that necessitated being physically taken care of, using drugs which worried the parents, and getting into predicaments and dramatic crises which called for a rescue. With maturity, though, and some psychoanalytic help, some of the neurotic self-destructive urges were resolved, and the person began getting attention in more positive twelfth house ways, by gradually becoming a spiritual teacher.

"Self-undoing" is a term much bandied about by astrologers in connection with the twelfth. It has to do with self-defeat or the ways you undermine yourself and act as your own worst enemy. For those wanting to understand this problem and its treatment better, I would highly recommend a book by Samuel J. Warner called, *Self-Realization and Self-Defeat* (paperback, Grove Press, 1966). The sign and planets in the twelfth plus the position of its ruler can show you how you are your own worst enemy. For example, Richard Nixon has Leo on the twelfth house and his ego was certainly his undoing, so much so that he was called "King Richard" by his critics.

I don't want to leave you with the impression that the twelfth is a negative house, because it has great power for good when we learn to stop using it destructively. In one of his beautiful analogies, Rod Chase points out that at sunrise the Sun comes up over the ascendant and travels through the twelfth house. This means that when we shine our light on the hidden things of the twelfth a new spiritual awakening will dawn. It may shine on materials hidden in the unconscious, on hidden spiritual teachings, and on people hidden away in prisons, institutions, or ghettos who need our help. At any rate, the positive use of twelfth house planets is to shine that light either for ourselves or for others.

CHAPTER 14

HOW TO ANALYZE ASPECTS FOR YOURSELF

An aspect is an angular relationship between two planets —30°, 60°, 90° and so on. The type of connection between the planets is determined by the nature of the angle. Aspects greatly modify the interpretation of a planet in a sign. For example, Mars in Virgo is hardly orderly if it's conjunct Neptune, but it is far more compassionate than Mars in Virgo is reputed to be. A Moon in Leo with Pluto nearby is a Leo Moon with a vengeance—a Scorpio-type vengeance, that is—but also with a Scorpio-type capacity for analysis.

There are many positive, modern books around today that will take you through each planet in all its possible aspects to each other planet. Nonetheless, if you rely primarily on books to analyze aspects, you'll be stuck with memorizing material from someone else, and you won't develop confidence in your own ability to put things together. What I'd like you to learn is to analyze the aspect in a chart first, and then, if needed, look it up to verify your work. Hopefully, this chapter will give you the tools to do that kind of analysis. Another drawback to relying on a book, no matter how good, is that the signs and houses the planets are in have to be taken into account for a truly valid interpretation, and none of the books can encompass that much material. To give an example of what I mean, a Moon in Scorpio squaring Jupiter in Aquarius is certainly going to be very different from a Moon in Sagittarius squaring Jupiter in Virgo, yet all most books can give you is the generalized interpretation of what it means to have the Moon square Jupiter.

Those Heavenly Orbs

Just as I didn't recommend any specific house system in the section on houses, neither will I make any recommendations on how wide or how narrow your orbs should be in computing aspects. I'm assuming you'll make your own decision on both, and my concern is in helping you learn to interpret. (For the uninitiated, orbs and house systems are a favorite battleground for the feuds between astrologers—smoke screens, I'm convinced, for the real question of Who's on Top.) I would make three suggestions for establishing whether any two planets are within orb of an aspect. First, be somewhat flexible, since a wider orb is sometimes indicated, particularly with the Sun, Moon, a stationary planet, planets near the angles, and planets completing a configuration like a t-square or a grand trine. Second, when in doubt, analyze the aspect and see if it is operating in the person's life. Third, the closer the aspect, the more strongly active it is in the person's life.

Richard Ideman has an interesting system he calls "planetary dialogues," which makes the question of orbs less important. He feels two planets in wide aspect or not aspecting at all can still be strongly connected by being in each other's house, sign, or in a number of other ways. This idea explained to me why a six-degree square from Mercury to Neptune in my chart, which should have been too weak to have much effect, left me the proverbial absent-minded professor. Mercury and Neptune are connected in three additional ways besides the weak square: 1) Mercury is on the cusp of the twelfth—Neptune's natural house, 2) Neptune is in the third—Mercury's natural house, and 3) Neptune is in Virgo—a Mercury-ruled sign. The more dialogues two planets have, the stronger the link, despite the amount of orb.

The Basic Meanings of the Aspects

Conjunction: ♂ (Two planets close together in the zodiac.) In most cases planets in conjunction are also in the same house and sign, so they have a great deal in common. They operate in a similiar way (same sign) and they are focused on the same area of life (same house). They are blended together in a way that makes them lose their autonomy, and whether a conjunction is "good" or "bad" depends on whether the two planets are basically friendly and harmonious toward one another. (Mercury and Jupiter are simpatico; Mars and Saturn are not.) The closer the conjunction, the more they are intermingled and forced to act together. A conjunction is a powerful aspect, and when you have several planets strung together in a series of conjunctions, it is even more powerful. Two or more planets out of the ten are acting out of the same space, and, as one of my students said, "That's a lot of volts coming out of one area of the zodiac."

Let's analyze a conjunction. A person may have Mercury and Neptune in Libra in the tenth house. Mercury is communication, while Neptune is intuition, but also haziness and confusion; the person may have good psychic ability, but has to work on communicating in ordinary spoken English. Mercury is writing and thinking, Neptune is creative, and Libra is concerned with beauty; so we can have a poet or writer. On the most negative level, Mercury is amoral and Neptune can be fraudulent; so we might have a swindler or a garden variety liar. The tenth house is the career of the person, so we could have anything from a fine poet to a famous psychic to a career con man. Here, as in all chart analysis, you have to get a sense of the rest of the chart, the person's spiritual level, and how the person is putting the aspect to use.

Sextile: ✳ (60° or two signs apart.) Complementary elements are usually involved in the sextile—water with earth and fire with air. Planets in sextile, then, can complement or enhance each other in some ways, each one filling in something the other lacks. Taurus, for instance, lends practicality to Pisces' other-worldliness, while Pisces' ability to flow and bend with conditions can offset Taurus' stubborn resistance to change. In practice, however, I pay very little attention to sextiles and give them a stingy orb— maybe because the people who have them don't pay much attention to them either. When I point out the talent a particular sextile brings, the person's reaction is often, "Oh, that." It's the taken-for-granted ability which the person often fails to make much use of—not something dynamic to mobilize and hone to a fine perfection. In transit, a sextile to a natal planet represents an opportunity which we, again, often fail to take advantage of because of lack of drive.

There are even some cases where two planets in sextile can bring out the worst in each other.[1] Take a Mercury in Aries sextile to Jupiter in Gemini. An Aries-Gemini combination could literally be hot air. Gemini has a million and one ideas but is more talk than action, and Aries has a lot of trouble finishing all those projects they start. Put the two together, and as fast as Aries gets going on one project, Gemini has dreamed up another one just as fascinating; the two in combination might not get much of anything done. Or, take a Virgo-Scorpio combination: both signs can be critical, perfectionistic, over-analytical, and want to make others over in their own image. Put the two together, and you've got not a Virgo but a virago . . . somebody pretty difficult to live with. Okay, all sextiles don't have to work out so negatively, but I do feel their beneficial effects are rather overrated.

Square: ☐ (90° or three signs apart.) Squares represent two urges or needs in a head-on conflict. They have a bad name in astrology that is not entirely deserved. Squares are the energizing forces within a person—the needs that drive them on. A person with many trines and sextiles but no squares often lacks the motivation to achieve their potential. Actually, conjunctions can be more destructive than squares, when the planets in question work together in an undesirable way. I would much rather see Venus square Saturn than Venus conjunct Saturn. Likewise, Mars square Neptune is easier to work out than Mars conjunct Neptune. With the conjunction, the undesirable condition is present constantly and the person has difficulty in visualizing any other outcome to their efforts. With the square, the action is intermittent, alternating, so it is easier to conceive of a positive result and the person is more able to mobilize inner resources in a new way. The square is dynamic, while the conjunction can be stagnant.

1. An idea developed more fully in my article, "What's so Great about a Sextile?", *American Astrology*, 7/75, v. 43:5, p. 45.

Let's try analyzing a square, so these ideas will become clearer. A person has Venus in Aries in the fifth house square Mars in Cancer in the eighth. The fifth house is romance, the eighth sexuality. Venus in Aries in the fifth indicates that the person is very romantic, the type to be forever chasing some new conquest. However, Mars in Cancer in the eighth could mean that our subject is quite insecure sexually, their performance dependent on moods and emotions, thus resulting in a great fear of rejection. The combination of this Mars and this Venus could make for a puzzling Don Juan type who conquers but never goes through with it. Supposing this combination were yours, how could it be made more comfortable? At least try conquering some shy but sensitive Cancerian who will understand your moodiness and insecurity and who will adore helping you to get over your own true shyness. Ah, but you say, the Cancer would cling and make your Venus in Aries fidget. Well, then you'd need to program some freedom into the relationship; work at making the person feel so secure about your love that they don't get threatened when you flirt. That devoted Cancer back home can even become a marvelous excuse for why you can't go through with that divine flirtation you've been carrying on all evening. So that no one gets hurt by it, you should only be flirting with others who enjoy it as a sport, but don't take it seriously.

The example above gives some ideas on how to resolve a square and make it easier to live with. See it as two of your children struggling for your attention. If you give both of them equal time and attention and assure both of them they are important to you, then neither will feel so slighted that they have to act up. It is hard to make both happy in one sitting, because they are so different, but if Johnny knows Billy is having time with you now but he'll have his own time with you later, he'll be more cooperative. Say, for instance, you have Sun in Taurus square your Moon in Aquarius. You have to find a way for both of them to be happy before you can be at peace with yourself. The Sun in Taurus has to have stability and security, but not at the cost of the Moon in Aquarius' need for freedom and non-conformity. Fully expressed, you might be the insurance salesman who is a wild motorcyclist on weekends, or some other arrangement might be made that allows both sides of your nature to be fulfilled. The important thing is not to make a value judgement that says one or the other side of the square is "bad" and that you shouldn't want or need to be like that.

Trine: △ (120° or four signs apart.) When planets are in a trine, they are usually in the same element—e.g., from water sign to water sign or from air sign to air sign. Since signs in the same element have many similar traits, needs, and abilities, the two planets enhance each other and do not create resistance or friction. The two planets work together cooperatively for the same ends. With a trine, there is a nice sense of flow and ease.

Take a trine in air, such as Moon in Libra and Mars in Gemini. All the air signs have a need to communicate and to circulate freely among numbers of people. The Moon in Libra produces a romantic who is in love with love all the time and not happy alone. Mars in Gemini puts a lot of energy into socializing, communicating and conquering people with words. The two together produce a charmer who needs people and knows exactly how to win them over. The two planets cooperate nicely, and the person has an easy time fulfilling their needs in this area. The problem, of course, is that if things are too easy for us, we tend not to work hard at them or to do much with them. Too many trines or sextiles can lead to laziness. The person with a Grand Trine (planets in all three signs in one element, all in aspect to one another) often has many abilities and many things falling into their lap, but may lay back and do nothing with all that potential. People with T-squares and Grand Crosses (patterns full of difficult aspects) generally achieve far more because they are more driven. You will see the truth of this if you study the charts of people who have accomplished worthwhile things.

The Semisquare (45°) ∠ **and Sesquiquadrate** (135°) ⚼ : These are commonly called "minor" aspects, but I find them fully as strong as squares both in natal charts and by transit. I experience the action of both aspects somewhat like a square, but more difficult to get a handle on. There is some agitation experienced in trying to make the two planets work together. The signs and houses involved don't really give you a clue to analyzing them because the signs could be either compatible or incompatible and so could the houses. Watch them, work with them, and you will probably come to agree that they are significant aspects. To find all possible semisquares and sesquiquadrates to a particular planet, move ahead one sign plus 15° (e.g., from 1° of Taurus to 1° of Gemini plus 15°; then, 16° Gemini is semisquare 1° Taurus.) Next, look to all four signs of that quadruplicity for the rest of the semisquares and sesquiquadrates. (Gemini is a mutable sign, so also look for planets at 16° Virgo, 16° Sagittarius, and 16° Pisces, all of which are mutable signs.)

The quincunx (or inconjunct): ⚻ (150° or five signs apart.) In my mind, the quincunx is also wrongly labelled a "minor" aspect. I observe it acting in people's lives in a profound and often fairly painful way. This holds true whether the quincunx is in the natal chart of the individual or is formed by a transit. The aspect usually involves two signs that are absolutely at odds with each other.[2] For instance, Leo and Capricorn are quincunx and truly make an odd couple. Leo is extremely social and extroverted, while Capricorn is reserved, not inclined to trust people, and introverted. Leo is generous to a fault, and Capricorn is thrifty (should we say tight?). Both Leo and Capricorn want recognition and power, it is true, but Leos believe they were born to rule and get highly insulted if you expect them to earn their throne, while Capricorn knows you have to climb the mountain step by laborious step. Leo wants life to be constant sunshine, and gloomy Capricorn is bound to rain on Leo's parade.

The quincunx also involves house matters that are difficult to reconcile. For instance, combining the fifth and the

2. This aspect was explored in greater depth in my article, "The Enigma of the Quincunx: Resolve Your Inner Conflicts," *American Astrology*. 1/76; v. 43:11, p. 22.

tenth has you trying to mix business with pleasure; the third and the eighth has you trying to do your homework while you've got loving on your mind, and the second and the seventh has you looking for a millionaire to marry. Some of the people can do some of these things some of the time, but by and large it's difficult. Don't neglect a consideration of the houses involved when you're trying to analyze a quincunx. With the quincunx, a tension is generated that often requires a dynamic and creative solution. Janis Joplin had Mercury in Aquarius quincunx her Moon in Cancer; the paradox was resolved by her electrifying, modernistic music, wherein she expressed her chaotic emotions. Woody Allen's wacky humor is partly explained by his Mercury in Sagittarius quincunx Uranus in Taurus; he pokes fun at the establishment in gentle ways. In many people, then, the necessity of reconciling two planets in quincunx forces a creative solution.

Opposition: ☍ (180° or six signs apart.) The opposition is another aspect that has a bad name in astrology, but which can have positive effects. The signs opposite each other are compatible in two ways: they are in complementary elements (fire is opposite air and earth is opposite water) and they operate in the same modality (cardinal is opposite cardinal and so on). Being face to face, the opposite signs give a certain ability to see both sides of the picture and to gain perspective on the self. When used properly, opposite signs can complement and fulfill each other. Cancer loves taking care of people, even when nobody asked them, and Capricorn wants to be cared for but would never admit to it; both signs are strongly motivated by security. Gemini loves to ask questions and Sagittarius thinks they know all the answers; both enjoy mental pursuits. Aries wants to lead and Libra is looking for a leader; both need someone else in order to feel complete. In all three cases, both signs fulfill needs the opposite sign has. When the two ends of the opposition alternate, there is a give and take like two children on a teeter-totter. When both ends stubbornly insist on their own way, the game changes to tug-of-war, and you reach an impasse.

That's when an opposition means trouble. Rightly used, this aspect requires the development of cooperation and mutuality.

Suppose that you have Moon in Pisces opposite Mars in Virgo. Pisces is creative, but would like to drift and dream, while Virgo wants to work endlessly on fine details. By alternating, you have both inspiration and perspiration . . . the two requirements of genius. Another opposition would be Saturn in Capricorn and Jupiter in Cancer. Saturn in Capricorn is all business, while Jupiter in Cancer is home and family oriented. If not in harmony, the person could be homesick while at work and preoccupied with job worries while at home. If both needs are given their due, you get a more well-balanced individual who is able to function effectively in two very different but related realms.

Steps in Analyzing Aspects

Many students of astrology feel at sea when confronted with two planets in aspect. Aspects are complex, and the only way to make them understandable is to break them down into their component parts, analyze them separately, and then combine and synthesize them. First, work on understanding each of the planets separately. Think about its basic nature (e.g., the connection of Mars with anger, competition, and sexuality), and how that planet is modified by the sign and house it is in. A Mars in Virgo, for instance, is much different than a Mars in Gemini. A Mars in the twelfth is focused on very different kinds of things than Mars in the tenth. So, first, understand the full meaning of that particular planet in that particular sign and house. Then do the same for the second planet in the aspect. Write both down in table form, if need be. Then begin putting the two together, combining the two planetary energies, the two signs, and the two houses involved plus the houses those planets rule. Finally, synthesize all the separate parts to see the dynamics.

An example may make things clearer. A chart shows Moon in Aries in the tenth, trine Mars in Leo in the first.

To get a grasp on what's involved, you might first want to make a table of the meanings of the Moon, the tenth house, and Aries, like the one below:

Table 1:

Moon	Tenth House	Aries
mothering	career	independent
women	achievement	energetic
security	status	aggressive
emotions	authority	competitive
dependency	long-range plans	fresh, vital
moods		always seeking the new

Then, somewhat like a child's school workbook, you'd combine each of the meanings of the Moon with each of the meanings of the tenth house. In the table below, I've taken just one of the Moon's key meanings, but to get a full understanding of the Moon in the tenth, you'd do it with each of the things the Moon represents.

Table 2:

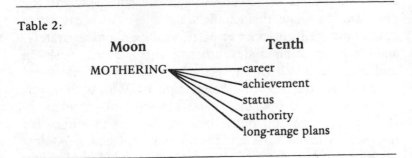

What picture emerges from this match-up? To combine mothering and career suggests the individual had a working mother and also that the individual's own career might involve taking care of others in some way. To combine mothering and achievement suggests the mother was competent and also perhaps that she pushed the individual to achieve, giving more mothering when the child was successful. The combination of mothering and authority produces an authoritarian mother. Mother combined with long-range goals produces a mother who could plan ahead and slowly work toward accomplishing something; the individual learned this trait also and can apply it to life. All put together we get the individual who has a great need for accomplishment and status, and who had a driving, ambitious mother. (In many ways, Moon in the tenth is like Moon in Capricorn.)

Moving ahead, but sticking with the mothering side of the Moon, let's see what we can learn by matching it up with the sign Aries, as in the table:

Table 3:

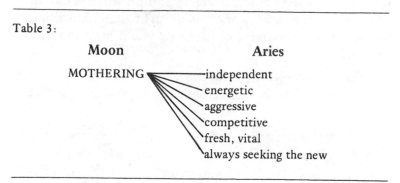

Here, the picture that emerges is of a mother who was aggressive and competitive, who pushed the child to be independent, who worked energetically, but with constantly changing focus. Hardly the type to develop serenity and security in the child, right? Combining the meanings of the Moon in Aries and the Moon in the tenth gives you a mother who was very much career and status oriented, who was authoritarian and fairly aggressive about it, who was too wrapped up in her own goals and drives to allow the child a normal amount of dependency. As a result, the individual also becomes rather driven to achieve, a competitive person who may even be using the arena of career to out-do the mother.

This much we have learned from just one of the key meanings of the Moon—mothering. As you see from Table 1, there are a number of other very critical functions the Moon plays in our lives. To get a full understanding of the Moon in Aries in the tenth, you'd make connections between each of the meanings of the Moon, each of the meanings of the tenth, and each of the meanings of Aries. Briefly, let's look at some possible combinations. The Moon is emotions and security, the tenth is the career, and Aries is independent and energetic. Here is an individual who feels insecure unless working hard at a career. Career is a very emotional area in the life—never "just a job." There is a dependence-independence conflict (mother never allowed dependency) which causes the person to feel unsafe in relying on anyone but themselves and on whatever accomplishments their hard work has brought them. Much more meaning can be found, but for that, you'll have to rely on yourself.

The second factor in the aspect was Mars in Leo in the first house. Below is a table with the key meanings of this placement.

Table 4:

Mars	First House	Leo
independence	outward personality	regal
energy	first impressions	passionate
competition	self-expression	self-involved
self-assertiveness	first years of life	life-affirming;
sexuality (conquest)	physical body	pleasure-loving
	appearance	generous
		sunshiny, warm
		vain, proud

To get a full picture of this Mars placement, you'd proceed as we did with the Moon. For the sake of brevity, however, let's scan the three columns. Mars in Leo in the first produces a strong personality, a fiery, dramatic, self-assertive person who loves having a good time and plenty of attention. Here is a proud, competitive person who can be quite aggressive. Nonetheless, the pride, dignity, and even laziness of Leo can keep Mars from being too sharp and hostile. Leo is a mellower sign that tempers the aggression of Mars. All in all, however, I'd say Mars in Leo in the first is an individual you can't push around.

Table 5:

Key Meaning of Aspect

Moon in Aries in the tenth trine Mars in Leo in the first

Moon	Tenth	Aries	Trine	Mars	First	Leo
mothering	career	independent	ease of expressing,	independence	outward	regal
women	achievement	energetic	mutual	energy	personality	dramatic
security	authority	aggressive	enhancement,	aggression	first	passionate
emotions	long-range plans	competitive	flow of energy,	competition	impressions	self-involved
dependency		changeable	wisdom, under-	self-assertiveness	self-expression	generous
moods			standing,	sexuality	physical body	life-affirming
habits			learning from		appearance	pleasure-loving
			experience		first year of life	sunshiny, warm
						vain, proud

The full aspect was Mars in Leo in the first trine Moon in Leo in the tenth. Table 5 reproduces the meanings of both plus the meaning of the trine aspect. Putting it all together, we come up with a winner, an individual who has many of the traits needed for success . . . ambition, energy, drive, competitiveness, and long-range planning. The trine helps the individual's boundless energy (Mars in the first) channel itself productively into the career (tenth). The Leo in the first/Moon in the tenth combination makes for a person who is naturally seen by others as an authority and a person to respect. The drawback of this marvelous-sounding aspect is that it can definitely be too much of a good thing—the aggressiveness can be overwhelming to others. The person may be too intent on their own goals to see the effect they have on others. You get a driving careerist who may not leave enough time for personal and social development in other areas of life.

This analysis has been a rather long process, and one that you may not need or want to undertake with every aspect that comes your way. However, if you are stuck on an aspect and feel you can't possibly understand what it means, it can be useful. Also, as you get more experience in astrology, the process goes on automatically in your head, without the need to write it down. A final consideration in analyzing aspects is the importance of understanding that the same aspect can work on various levels, from the most concrete and material to the deepest psychological and spiritual. For instance, I found an aspect in my chart that explains why I have never had many electrical appliances in my home (Venus, ruler of my fourth, conjunct Saturn and Uranus), but the same aspect also has extremely profound implications that clarify my relationships. The fascinating thing about astrology is that you continue to get deeper and deeper insights into yourself as you go along.

"Afflictions" & "Bad Aspects"

People who are into astrology are always crying over the "bad aspects" in their charts. "My Venus is afflicted, so I'll never have love." "If Saturn weren't square my Mars, I could do so much more." "This grand cross is killing me! What karma I must have to deserve it!" This is a cop-out use of astrology—putting the blame on your aspects rather than yourself.[3] The chart only describes you and your character, rather than being some malevolent fate outside yourself controlling you. If your Mars is "afflicted" (a word I dislike), it can mean merely that you are a person who deals with anger in unhealthy or inappropriate ways. Rather than giving up, you should be looking to the chart to tell you what you need to work on in dealing with anger. You aren't being put upon by karma, you are only being shown (or even pushed toward) the road to a healthier, stronger character. Difficult aspects, natally or by transit, are often the things that drive us to accomplish something, that mobilize us to change, and that keep us from settling into inertia. Likewise, it is adversity in life (the outward manifestation of difficult aspects) that pushes us to achieve worthwhile things. For instance, the loss of a child to a disease like muscular dystrophy has spurred the founding of several national child health organizations. The experience itself was tragic and painful, but the end result was something positive and constructive. Take a longer view of your bad aspects, and try to understand what strengths and accomplishments have come out of the discomfort these aspects produce.

Take the example of a Venus-Saturn aspect. This indicates over-seriousness in young people, which generally doesn't make them popular with their own age group. Such persons instead are often studious and form relationships with people older than themselves who teach them a great deal and who often have a positive effect on their career. While it is painful for teenagers not to feel at ease with their peers, much that is worthwhile often comes out of their solitary studies and their friendships with older people. Also, age helps bring out the positive side of this aspect— the person is a late bloomer, but matures gracefully and ages slowly.

---

3. These ideas were explored more fully in my article, "Bad Aspects—The Big Cop-out," *American Astrology*, 12/75, v. 43:10, p. 25.

Another point to consider with your so-called bad aspects is that every planetary aspect, like every sign and house placement of a planet, has a positive and constructive use that you can put it to, if you study and discover it. For instance, I knew a woman with Mars in Aries quincunx Venus in Virgo who put a great deal of energy into organizing slum kids into baseball teams which her church sponsored, with good effects on all concerned. The more you can focus on the uplifting level of both of the planets in the aspect, the less energy you have left to devote to pursuing the negative consequences.

If you have a "bad aspect" in your chart, pin it up on your wall and study and meditate on it intensely for a few months. Trace the ways it operates in your life, on many different levels. Without passing the buck, find out the part you play in the problems it creates. List the concrete steps you can take to change what you're doing to create those problems. Ask yourself what strength or compensations you've developed as a result of the aspect. (I call them side benefits—if you don't find any, you're either not looking deeply enough or you're working it out totally on a negative level.) Think about the most positive possibilities of those two planets in their sign and house, and work toward achieving that. If you do this seriously with each aspect in your chart, it will accelerate your growth and increase your happiness and self-confidence.

PART FOUR
ASTROLOGY AT WORK

CHAPTER 15

A SPIRITUAL & PSYCHOLOGICAL PERSPECTIVE ON TRANSITS

In earlier chapters we dealt simultaneously with a planet and its transits. They cannot be separated, for without a thorough understanding of a planet and what it represents both generally and in the chart of a particular individual, you cannot understand its transits. This chapter, however, contains more specific information about my approach to transits and my view of their purpose in our lives.[1] You may wonder why there is nothing about progressions in this book. Some respected astrologers use progressions exclusively and get good results from them, but I personally find transits more meaningful and choose to use them exclusively. For, in order to achieve depth in any area of astrology, we must *focus* rather than scatter ourselves all over the zodiac.

The Outer Planets

We will concentrate on the outer planets—Saturn, Uranus, Neptune, and Pluto—since they are the truly powerful ones with the most lasting effects. Transits by the Moon, Mercury, Venus, Mars, and Jupiter represent the small changes and activities of our daily lives, ephemeral at best. (Notice the common root word shared by *ephemeral* and *ephemeris*. Ephemeral means lasting for only a day. An *emphermerid* is a May fly, a species which lives a very short life.) Transits by the outer planets, on the other hand, mark the deeply meaningful periods in our lives, in which we make profound changes in ourselves and our environment. The truly significant connections we make with our universe, the ones that lift us out of our day-to-day routine and make us the persons we are, are shown by the outer planets.

Astrologers of the old school generally have a gloomy, fearful outlook on transits by the outer planets, seeing the

---

1. The greater part of this chapter originally appeared in Dell Horoscope Magazine, in the September and October, 1975 issues, as "A Spiritual-Psychological Approach to Transits." It is reprinted with their permission. © 1975 by Dell Publishing Co., Inc.

resulting event or conditions as done to us by some powerful, malevolent external force. In actuality, a transit by an outer planet is a challenge and an opportunity to grow and develop. It exaggerates what is already within you (you have the planet in your natal chart somewhere), and it forces the issue, so that you have to deal with it. By studying our charts, we can find out what the lesson might be and *work with* the transit rather than against it. Working against or opposing change means having to learn the hard way, which can be painful.

The outer planets move very slowly, and I think this long exposure is necessary because their lessons are so difficult to learn. (Pluto and Neptune transits are the slowest and are also, in my opinion, usually the most difficult.) Besides moving slowly, they generally pass over the same degree of the zodiac three times, due to their apparent retrograde motion. This gives us three opportunities to grow in that particular area of life. You generally find people rather overwhelmed by the first cross-over, working at it on the second, and resolving it on the third, although the process of adjustment goes on throughout. You may also see repeated transits by the same planet to one after another of your natal planets which fall near the same degree (e.g., you may have several planets at 15° of different signs). This sort of hammering away seems to force us to learn a particular lesson in a hurry. We keep having transits by a planet so long as we still have something to learn from it . . . and how easily we forget; so we often have to relearn, like repeating a grade in school. We also may have to relearn the same thing at differing levels of awareness or in different areas of our lives. Or, we might be having one last fling with a particular problematical behavior pattern that isn't yet completely removed from our lives, in order to convince ourselves how miserable that behavior makes us.

Transits & Personal Responsibility

People who study astrology are fond of saying things like, "I went through a terrible time when Pluto crossed my

Sun, but I'VE REALLY LEARNED MY LESSON!" These avowals of spiritual progress used to impress me, until I began to notice that many people who said this hadn't changed at all. They might avoid the original situation that caused them so much misery, but they would plunge right into a similar one that was just as self-destructive. I finally concluded that "I've really learned my lesson," was just a bit of karmic chic or a hip way of saying, "How I've suffered!" Real progress comes only when you carefully evaluate your part in the situation—why you got into it, what neurotic needs it met, where you fell down, and how such difficulties can be avoided in the future. Blaming others, rather than seeing your own part in it, is a sure sign you haven't really learned anything at all. Blaming the planets for your problems is another sign that you're not taking responsibility for yourself. The notion that you are being buffeted by Uranus or held back by Saturn is very short-sighted. As we saw in the chapter on houses, we attract events, conditions and people to ourselves because of our own inner conflicts, needs, beliefs, and attitudes, whether they be conscious or unconscious. Erroneous or misguided patterns of thought and action are at the root of most of our troubles. Start examining your own thoughts, actions, and emotions in your problem areas and during difficult transits to see how you contribute to or provoke the "mistreatment" you get from the planets.

Let's say that you've been overly self-indulgent in some way . . . like running up your charge accounts. Then Saturn begins transiting your second house and you have to pay . . . and pay . . . and pay. Do you blame Saturn for your fiscal crunch? Or do you put the responsibility back where it belongs . . . on yourself? For another example—you just can't pull yourself together in the morning and you keep getting to work later and later. Then one fine day Uranus squares your Midheaven and you find yourself without a job. Do you blame that awful Uranus? How about blaming yourself for all the times you decided to sleep just fifteen minutes later? Don't pass the buck onto the transiting planets. The responsibility for our lives as adults rests fully and completely on our own shoulders. Saturn is called "the Reaper," but to some extent all the transiting planets indicate that you have to reap what you've already sown. If you've sown diligently, you'll reap the benefits of it.

So, why do we need to study our transits? Because they are a tool to help us become more conscious and evolved, more aware of ourselves and our reactions, and more insightful. Following your transits intelligently and responsibly can bring into focus the situations and conditions you find yourself in, and help you to analyze your part in it. Rightfully, they should be used for study rather than divination and regarded as useful signposts, rather than disruptions by malevolent forces.

Transits as Process

Transits are not isolated events over which you have no control but are instead part of a psychological process within yourself which they reflect. Too much attention is paid in astrology to events and not enough to the processes that bring them about. Actually, events are like signposts— more visible than the process, naturally, but when you're traveling, you don't jump from one town to the next, you cover the distance gradually. Thus it is with events in your life . . . you get there gradually via an internal psychological process. Transit readings that focus only on events miss out on a potent tool for self-knowledge and change.

When I do a yearly reading for a client, I first try to get an idea from her of what has been going on in the last year because this helps me grasp the specific process indicated by a transiting planet. Let's say that Neptune began a long transit to her Mercury last year and will continue into the coming year. I can suggest a number of things that may be going on; but when the client pinpoints it, it is more useful because it shows how she is using Neptune in her life. More accurately, it indicates how she is *beginning* to use it because transits often show a *transit*ion to another, generally healthier, way of using a planet's energies. With this kind of feedback, I can relate coming transits to the specific processes already in motion, judging when they might come to a critical stage and when they might begin to be resolved. I can also point out ways of working with the processes if they are healthy for the person or more constructive channels for the planet's energies if they are not. Predictions made in this way may not be as spectacular as the shot-in-the-dark variety, but they are more organically related to the client's life.

Analyze some of the events of your life in terms of the processes that lead up to them and you will get much more insight into them. Let's go back to the example of being fired under a Uranus transit. You may have been restless and wanting to change jobs for a while (Uranus), so you developed progressively worse work habits which ultimately got you fired. Or you may have been going through a period of rebellion against authority (Uranus again), and you'd been pushing your luck pretty far with the boss. These are both Uranus-type processes that might lead to the Uranus-type event of getting fired. To give another example, a couple I know have both been under heavy Pluto transits for some time. They have been through quite a bit of therapy during this period and now feel for the first time that they are ready for parenthood. Both therapy and pregnancy are Plutonian processes, but all the outside world will recognize is the Plutonian event—the birth of a child. The inner psychological processes, however, are what lead up to the actual outer event. Once again, we see the metaphysical truth that the person's outer world reflects and is created by their inner world.

It is helpful, too, to understand life as a process that you are participating in and have some control over rather than as a series of unconnected events. Your participation may not be overly clear to you, as you may be doing these things unconsciously rather than consciously. This is where the study of psychology is a useful adjunct to astrology. Together they can act as a guide to help you take better control of your life. Events, then, may be the culmination of a process, but they can also be a catalyst that starts another process in motion. True, they can be quite painful; but it is often the painful situation that forces us to grow in spite of ourselves. Only the pinch of necessity moves us out of our inertia into changing our lives for the better. Without the energy hard transits give us, we'd be likely to stagnate and to go on making the same mistake endlessly. A destructive relationship, for instance, can drag on for years without either party having the will to break it off— until Uranus brings it to a head. Naturally, one is upset at the parting; but after a while, both are free to grow in ways the relationship prevented before. Whether they do grow or whether they hurry into another destructive relationship depends on their insight, but at least the freedom to grow is there.

We have seen a number of reasons transits need to be considered as processes, giving events their due place and nothing more. If you will examine some of the events in your life this way, trying to retrace the emotional process that preceded them or followed them, you will see more clearly how such events are related to the actual course of your life. Seen in an isolated context, an event may appear to be a totally unprovoked disaster. Tracing the process, however, you can see more of how you contributed to it and what its effects have been on your life as a whole. You may be surprised to find that the net result was actually quite positive, as in the case of many divorced women who relied too heavily on their husbands and who are now stronger and more independent than they were before the divorce.

The Natal Chart — Key to Transits

I am indebted to my teacher, Richard Ideman, who impressed on me the truth that you cannot understand transits unless you have a deep knowledge of the natal chart. In my view, the natal chart is the cosmic plan for our development, complete at birth but unfolding through transits. Different parts of us, different abilities and strengths, are developed at different times of our lives through our experiences. One part may not be able to develop meaningfully until another has reached a certain level of strength. We may get tired of waiting for something or think the timing of an event was bad, but we can't see far enough to view the whole plan. It is not *our* timing that is being followed but God's. It is a perfectly choreographed dance—Saturn waiting in the wings until Neptune has done its work, and so on. To understand a transit and its potentialities, you have to go deeply into the natal chart and examine the natal-chart function of both the transiting planet and the planet being transited. For example, if Neptune is transiting your Mars, you have to take into account how both Mars and Neptune operate in your chart—by sign and house positions, rulerships, aspects, and general strength. The transit calls forth the conflicting problems related to these natal planets and makes you deal with them. It exaggerates certain tendencies and forces you to balance them out. Where something is comparatively weak in your chart, the transit acts as a booster shot to help you develop it. In other cases, it is like an overdose, bringing an already overly strong trait to a critical level where the person has to recognize it ("now that I have your attention") and to learn to deal with it in a more balanced way.

This may become clearer if we use an example. Suppose a woman has Venus and Neptune conjunct in the seventh house. This could express itself in picking partners of an undesirable type she thinks she can reform. Such a pattern of choices makes her vulnerable to exploitation and to being hurt when her unrealistic hopes for these people collapse. If Saturn or Pluto crosses that conjunction, it would doubtlessly be a heartbreaking time: maybe an incident where such a choice of partners backfired badly. Just possibly, however, such an event might bring her to stop this behavior once and for all. Unless she used it introspectively though, she might go into another kind of self-destructive situation, different on the surface but very much the same underneath. She might, for instance, stop going out with ex-convicts but start going out with alcoholics. (Both are Venus-Neptune types.) Or, she might stop relating completely.

A deep understanding of her part in the situation would be necessary before she would be able to make any real change. There is rarely such a thing as a totally innocent victim, especially when you see a repeated pattern of such events in a person's life. She would have to recognize that such partners didn't "just happen" to her; she unconsciously selected them because they met her needs in some way that caused her to blind herself to their true nature. (Some people get gratification, you know, from playing the martyr.) Maybe these men unconsciously made her feel quite superior and at the same time like a very special, terribly compassionate person who would work a miracle with such people. If this woman fully understood her part in her disastrous relationships and was willing to give up the gratification or find it in some less self-destructive way, she might be ready to select a different kind of partner. This would still have to be someone who fits the description of her seventh-house conjunction of Venus and Neptune, since it won't just go away. But that combination can describe some very positive partners, too . . . spiritual people, artists, or maybe a sweet and sensitive but together Piscean.

This, then, would be an example of using the transit to understand and to do something about a natal aspect that has probably been a thorn in your side all your life. Any attempt to understand transits without turning to the natal chart and to the behavior patterns behind it is bound to be shallow and not lead to a constructive or enduring change. Even when an event is painful and appears destructive on the outside, the end result will be constructive if you use it to put an end to a harmful pattern.

Some Thoughts on the Meaning of Pain

In order to make some sense of transits—and, in fact, to make some sense of life—we have to gain a deeper understanding of pain. Be it physical, emotional, mental or spiritual, pain is not always as bad as we think it is. Sometimes it is only a by-product of growth and change, and sometimes it is the only thing that will get us back on the road to health. Let me explain what I mean at greater length to see if you will agree with me.

I am not minimizing the pain that traumatic events or illness can bring—nor even the emotional agony we go through during a long transit of a planet like Pluto or Neptune. We all suffer greatly at such times. Nor am I saying that pain is desirable, because it almost always signifies that some part of our physical, mental, emotional, or spiritual nature needs realignment. But pain is the proverbial cry for help; if we heed it, if we do something constructive about it, we can prevent further complications and enter a healthier time of our lives. Some of the pain we experience might be regarded as "growing pains." Our bodies, as medicine is only starting to comprehend, have amazing powers of adjustment; and I suspect this is true of our minds as well. The runner who consistently stretches himself to achieve greater speed may have some pain in his tired muscles at first, but he soon can reach that speed in every race without being exhausted. Pain often comes during the process of readjusting to a greater demand, but the organism grows to accommodate the demand; soon the higher level of functioning is no longer painful, but actually feels normal to us. On the spiritual level, too, we may experience some pain as we try to stretch ourselves; but we soon function better than ever. It is often a hard transit that gives us the impetus to stretch ourselves or that provides the conditions under which we are forced to stretch ourselves if we are not doing so voluntarily.

PAIN IS WORTHWHILE IF IT ACCOMPLISHES SOMETHING—like the pain you feel after an operatiothat repairs or removes something that has been draining away your health for years. Psychotherapy, which is often entered into under a Pluto transit, also entails that kind of pain, as you purge from your unconscious things that have been holding you back most of your life. Facing up to facts you have suppressed can be painful, but it is often the only way to emotional health. The pain of such things is temporary, but the growth is long-lasting; similarly, women quickly forget the pains of giving birth to a child. Looked at from this point of view, a great deal of the pain of transits is, I believe, no more than a side effect of the process of strengthening, healing, and growing that goes along with any major transit. We err in focusing our attention on the pain rather than on the growth process and in letting the pain be what we remember. Concentrating on any kind of pain just makes it hurt more; this is the reason the doctor gives the child a lollipop. Sometimes in focusing on the pain, we don't see the growth at all—or we may see it in a kind of upside-down fashion, perceiving the growth as the side effect rather than the main purpose of the transit. "Well, I suffered terribly when my husband left me; but at least I learned to be independent." The important thing is the new independence, not the suffering. Look at some of the periods of your life when you suffered a great deal; try to find out what transit you were under; and try to trace what growth came of it.

One of pain's useful functions is as a flashing red light—a warning that something is wrong. Many people don't pay attention to a physical or emotional problem until it begins to hurt. If pain moves you to do something about the problem, it is a blessing in disguise because early action can prevent all kinds of what medicine calls "sequellae" (the "for want of a horse the kingdom was lost" effect). A Saturn transit, for example, might bring an illness; but the illness was not caused by Saturn. It is the result of your long-term self-neglect or self-abuse, such as eating the wrong things or not taking care of yourself properly. If you will call forth the positive Saturn traits during the transit and after (traits like self-discipline and taking responsibility for yourself), the transit can help you get back on the road to good health. If you do not use it in that way you are vulnerable to further deterioration of your health. This holds true with problems you might have on the emotional or spiritual level as well. If you are hurt by an event but use it to analyze the part of your chart involved in the transit, you can begin to change the behavior patterns that bring on such events, avoiding worse problems in the future. Thus, the emotional pain has served a useful purpose, no matter how unpleasant it was.

Some of our emotional pain is actually a kind of temper tantrum at not being given what we want when we want it. An occult teaching goes "Beware of your wishes." It seems to be a wise saying indeed because so many of the things we want desperately and agonize over not having would be quite terrible for us if we actually got them. Try to think back on some of the things you wanted with all your heart ten years ago and what your life would have been like if you'd achieved them. When I was a senior in college, I can remember being horribly depressed and humiliated because Columbia School of Social Work rejected me. I never thought for a moment how very difficult it would be for me as a naive, small-town Midwesterner to adjust to New York City; I only knew that my dreams had collapsed. Yet, several years later, when I actually did go to Columbia to finish my grad work, it was still an incredibly difficult adjustment despite my greater age and experience. I think that there is always a good reason why we don't get the things that we yearn for and that the reason will be clear to us later on if we look for it. I believe there is something at work which is far wiser than we are, that knows what is good for us and what is not, and that can see far enough into the future to know the best time for things to unfold. As Eastern philosophers say, "God's delay is not his denial."

Much of the pain of transits seems to come from resistance to change. We human beings are so bound up with inertia and with fear of the unknown that any change seems like a calamity to us. When you resist change or continue in behavior you know is self-destructive, it is like knocking your head against the wall—painful, but it is needless pain. Then, too, if we don't work willingly toward change, events happen that force revisions upon us. If we change voluntarily and work cooperatively with the transit, it is generally more productive and less painful.

Steps in Making Better Use of Your Hard Transits

The following are some suggested steps, which, over time, will help you make the most of each transit that comes your way. I realize they are rather sweeping and easier said than done in most cases. Yet, if you have read through to this point, you can doubtlessly see the logic behind them and can imagine the dividends they would pay were you able to put them to effective use in your life.

Step No. 1: *Get to know the planets well.* Study all the planets in depth; know their positive and negative meanings and uses and the psychological processes involved. Examine all of them, but focus especially on the ones affecting you by transit. One method of doing this is to go over the past events in your life and find out what transiting planets affected your chart then. See how you have reacted to a number of transits by a single planet. You can't completely judge from past transits, however, because they were affecting a different part of your chart then and you were, hopefully, a different person then, having grown through your last contact with the planet. Ultimately, your deepest understanding of the planets will come from monitoring yourself during present and future transits by all the planets and to all the planets in your chart.

Step No. 2: *Get to know your chart in real depth.* Seek to know and understand every part of your chart and what it represents in your life at present. Know the positive and the negative levels of expression of each house and sign placement and each aspect, both as you are now using them and in their greatest potential. Take inventory of yourself—what is being used in a good way, and where are you living out the negative use of a combination? How can you shift to more positive expression of your chart? What strengths and abilities could you have that you haven't yet developed? What is the real you and what have you let your culture, parents, and other social pressures talk you into being? All this shows in a deep analysis of your natal chart. A transit can bring out the best or the worst of a given aspect, depending on the current level of expression of the planets involved. Knowing all the potentials of each part of your chart can help you know what direction to head in during a transit. In effect, understanding your natal chart profoundly puts you into the driver's seat.

Step No. 3: *Take the long view of things.* Try to look at the results of the transit over the long haul; see the transits as TRANSITory. This will help you bear the pain better and spur you to make use of the opportunities while you still have them. During a transit, you may seem to yourself to be falling apart in some area; but you are often only integrating yourself on a deeper level and will be healthier than ever afterwards. You may just be seeing that certain things are really not as important as you once thought them to be, and so you are unwilling to invest your energies in them any longer. It may help to keep a journal of your innermost thoughts and feelings during heavy transits or a record of your dreams. Looking back on it afterwards, you can see the process more clearly than you do day by day or than relying on memory. It is like the growth of a pet or a child—so gradual that the people closest to it don't see it. Ask people who've known you for a period of time how you have changed.

Step No. 4: *Discard old notions in judging the effects of a transit.* Sometimes transits are only "bad" when judged by false concepts and values. Too often we evaluate what is happening to us from the standards of the masses rather than what is good for us personally in our current stage of development. Pluto transits, for example, often bring desire to withdraw inward and think deeply about the self. From the standpoint of the masses, this is "a bad sign" that you are becoming "socially maladjusted"—but introspection is needed for change and for doing creative work, so the Pluto transit may be just what you need to straighten yourself out. In our culture, people value only extroversion, social success, and "having fun"; but these are shallow accomplishments and leave nothing lasting, nor do they make you a stronger person. Leave the standards and values of the masses behind and judge the transit by what is going on inside you. Another type of old notion that you need to discard is your old self concepts. Don't let them paralyze you and hold you back when the transit impels you toward something new. Don't say, for instance, "I'm not the kind of person to teach a class," when you have the knowledge and the students are there clamoring for you to begin. Never be limited by your own or other people's definitions of yourself. We all have greater capacity than we have ever used.

Step No. 5: *When you have a lemon, make lemonade.* Use the transit to develop the positive potential of an aspect. This will help in two ways: 1) It will focus your attention away from the pain and thus lessen it; 2) It will divert some of the energy away from the self-destructive ways of behaving and help you "kick your habit," whatever it is. The more energy that is diverted into a positive expression, the less there is for the negative. The concept of "when you have a lemon, make lemonade" may be clearer if I give you an example. I have Venus and Saturn conjoined in my eleventh house. Neptune was opposite it for an entire winter, during which I had some severe disappointments and disillusionments about my friends. It was a lonely and depressing time, but I used those lonely winter days to learn about handicrafts (the conjunction is in Gemini). I had always felt rather inferior to artists and yearned to create beautiful things. In developing the skills of handicrafts, I accomplished this.

Step No. 6: *Avoid escapism.* In this culture, we think we have to feel good all the time or we take a drink, take a pill, or take a powder. Using a "pain killer"—be it physical or emotional—can keep you from really doing something about the problem that is causing the pain of that transit. Many use the pain as a stimulus not for growth, but for escapist behavior, like heavy drinking or drugs. Rather than learning not to be so self-destructive, they use the situation as an excuse for more drinking or other self-destructive pursuits. The man whose wife leaves him for beating her when he is drunk, for example, may use her leaving him as a reason to start drinking continually. The excuse types, to hear them tell it, are always the innocent victim—never seeing the suffering they caused or the ways they provoked what was done to them. Ask yourself honestly, and not in a breast-beating way, what did I do to deserve this? If you look honestly enough, you will find out.

Step No. 7: *Find out where the pain is coming from and do something about it.* There is a current saying, "Go with the pain"—meaning, experience it fully, don't tense up against it; work until you find out where it comes from. There seems to be much wisdom in this if we have the courage to do so. Seeking deep within your body, deep within your emotions, and deep within your soul to find out where that pain is coming from can help you work it out and purge it once and for all.

Summary

This chapter on transits has been meant to provide some ideas on the part transits play in our upward spiritual evolution, because even the most painful transits, properly used, can lead to growth. In order to analyze a specific transit to your chart or someone else's, you would need to combine and think over several parts of this book: the chapter on aspects, the chapter on houses, and the chapters on the two planets involved. The best book on transits currently available is Robert Hand's *Planets in Transit*,* (Para Research, 1976), a worthwhile investment for people who want to study astrology in greater depth.

*Available from CRCS Publications, the publisher of this book. (See address o▪ title page.)

CHAPTER 16

GAMES ASTROLOGERS PLAY

As more and more people begin to consult astrologers, there is great potential for twisted practitioners to do real harm. Clients tend to attribute great powers to astrologers because information about the most intimate parts of their lives seems to come from mysterious and even psychic sources. Real spiritual enlightenment is far from being the rule among astrologers. Unfortunately, there are many who are disturbed, neurotic, or outright charlatans. There are no professional standards or controls of any kind in the practice of astrology in most areas of the country at this time. Any one could pass himself off as an astrologer with no penalty.

Of course this does not mean you should avoid astrology altogether, for it is still an important path to self-awareness, and there are still many solid practitioners. It merely means that you should be watchful. If you have a really negative, shattering reading, it is more likely due to the emotional problems of the astrologer. Rather than sink into despair, look for someone who can give you a positive, constructive reading of your birth chart. (Rules and suggestions for finding a good astrologer are given later on in this chapter.) And astrologers themselves should examine closely *the images that they project.* Is the image really *helpful to the client*—or is it simply a mask to hide behind?

Destructive astrologers fall into certain personality groupings. The following descriptions, even though they are stereotypes, may help you avoid choosing one of them. Be very wary of:

The Cultist: Not to be confused with the true occultist, he tries to set himself up as some sort of god or guru. He tends to be theatrical and to make astrology look very mysterious. He thrives on slavish, devoted followers—generally female—who revere his every word and who never have any ideas of their own. All other astrologers are incompetent, and you are terribly lucky you came to him for the true word. If you doubt or question this "highly spiritual" person in any way, he will quickly become vindictive and make snide remarks about your Sun sign, your Saturn or your karma. He specializes in negative and moralistic interpretations of the chart. One of them told a friend of mine that she had the worst chart he'd ever seen, that she must have been a terrible person in her last life to deserve a chart like that, and that now the chickens were coming home to roost.

The "Astro-Analyst:" This one is also hungry for power over you, but is more modern, subtle, and more dangerous. They often claim a background in psychology when they may have no more than an introductory course. Their special gift is in finding your weaknesses and using them to gain a subtle psychological dependency through your guilt, anxiety, and self-doubts. They specialize in half-baked psychological diagnoses a trained expert would use cautiously. They feel many of their clients are latent homosexuals, have strong incestual desires, or are potentially schizophrenic. When you belatedly catch on to them and try to extricate yourself—watch out! The most subtle and devastating psychological warfare is their forte.

The Mother Hen: This type of astrologer is so fearful of "the stars" that she can scarcely be reassuring or give you any positive direction. She sees us all as puppets of big, evil forces in the sky who do things to us over which we have no control. She aids and abets that part of you that wants to use your chart as a cop-out for your behavior because "you were born that way." A real yenta, she is always telling you that you will regret not taking her advice when that next bad planet comes over. When you ask about the future, her anxious silences make you feel she is hiding something from you. She is—her ignorance! (Dane Rudhyar has called this type of astrologer the "lunar" type.)

The **Doom-Sayer**: These are found in all walks of life today, but in astrology they have more of a ring of authority because they can invoke the name of planetary influences. Not only is the world falling apart, but people are intrinsically evil, and you, dear client, are rotten to the core. Nothing good is going to happen to you for at least twelve years, and you must be prepared for the worst possible outcome of all transits. Your health is in peril and you can look forward to spending your last years in an institution. The karma you are reaping is formidable. If you are a bit of a doomsayer yourself, you will find this one very helpful in confirming your own worst fears.

The **Sweetie Pie**: Although totally negative astrologers can be very devastating, the totally positive astrologer is almost worthless. Unless your self-concept is so low that you need intravenous ego-support, what good does it do you to go to an astrologer who will only tell you the good things about yourself? This is a common fault of beginning students, Sun-sign books, and your best friend. Find someone strong enough to tell you like it is, even if it hurts a little. Real growth can only come through self-awareness— and self-awareness can be painful. The good astrologer will show you both the negative and positive sides of your chart and help you toward their constructive use.

The **Curious (Yellow) Astrologer**: There are astrologers your mother should have warned you about. They will tell you that you are sexually frustrated and hint that they are just the person to relieve you of that frustration. One told a friend of mine she would be a sex-maniac by the time she was thirty unless she found a good lover and almost simultaneously suggested he'd like to see more of her. Certainly sexual matters can be helpfully discussed in astrological consultation, although serious sexual problems require expert medical and psychological help. Some "astrologers," however, use the chart for their own prurient interest. Generally they are more of a nuisance than a danger, unless you take their readings seriously.

The Fortune-Teller: This modern-day gypsy preys on our desire to avoid anxiety about the uncertainty of the future by volunteering to help us plan every detail of our lives. To impress us with how well she knows us, she will divine such deathless matters as our letter-writing habits and our third cousin's divorce. Her predictions of the future have a similarly profound basis. They often come true, unfortunately, because of the well-known phenomenon of self-fulfilling prophecy. In India they tell the story of the man who became so frightened by an astrologer's prediction that he would die on a certain day that he shot himself to avoid the pain of death. Taking such prophecies seriously can make them happen, whether or not they are really "in the stars."

The Life of the Party: At nearly every party now, you will meet a self-styled "astrologer" who uses a very superficial knowledge of Sun signs to get the spotlight. It may also be a part of his line to make time with the attractive girls. These types are fond of making dire predictions like, "The next seven years are going to be bad for Geminis," or generic put-downs like, "Virgos are terrible people." Such statements are worse than nonsense, because they can be quite destructive. This type will usually squirm when you try to pin them down. Ask him if he knows how to set up a chart, if he's actually taken classes, and how long he's been studying. Unless he scores pretty high on these questions, don't take him seriously.

HOW TO FIND A GOOD ASTROLOGER: Personal recommendation of an astrologer by someone whose judgement you respect is probably the best way of finding an astrologer. Your local astrological organization may or may not be a good source—fairly often Mr. Cultist is the president of that organization. I would tend to be suspicious of astrologers who advertise—the best ones operate solely on the recommendations of their satisfied clients. You might find your astrologer by going to lectures on astrology and evaluating the speakers. In any case, you will probably have a preliminary interview, either by phone or in person, and you can ask for one if the astrologer does not. Use your own judgement during this contact, and if you feel the person you are speaking to fits into one of the categories described here or possibly just is not compatible with you, you can and should pull out before either of you invests more time and money.

HOW TO RECOGNIZE A GOOD ASTROLOGER: A good astrologer will avoid falling into the pitfalls described here. He has respect for your individuality and your potential and is mainly positive and constructive in his approach. Old-fashioned astrological ideas about good and evil planets and aspects are replaced with a balanced outlook. He welcomes your questions and ideas and looks for feedback about the correctness of his interpretation. He is not interested in controlling and dominating you but wants to help you find your own thing. He will not be your guru or your therapist or make your decisions or take away one iota of your responsibility for your own growth, but will show you where you are and how you can move to a higher level of functioning. A good astrologer, like a good friend, is a priceless thing.

CHAPTER 17

FROM BEDFORD-STUYVESANT TO THE STARS — BY SUBWAY

I walk eagerly up the long ramp to the alcohol treatment center, where I teach astrology as a volunteer. My class, made up of patients from the center, is going to Columbia University tonight to look through a telescope at some of the planets we've been studying.[1] Pausing at the top of the stairs, I check to see which planets are visible. Jupiter is nestled in the inner curve of the Moon, a big white twinkle light against the Moon's softer ivory. "We picked a good night," I think. "Cold, but so clear we'll be able to see a lot."

Happy, I push open the door, warm air and warm greetings enfolding me. "Hi, astrology teacher! How are you?" "Look who's here!" Hanging out in the hallway and around the front desk are some of the men I've already taught and others I know in passing. Fewer women than men come to the program, and most of the patients are Black—the center is in Bedford-Stuyvesant, Brooklyn.[2]

I smile and wave at them, as I stop to talk to Cheryl, the recreation director. She apologizes, "Sorry, but I can't go with the class tonight. Listen, when will you start a new class? So many of the patients are interested."

"I'm thinking about another beginning class in January. I'm really enjoying working with the students. Such insightful people!"

"Great!" Cheryl says. "Let me know when you're ready. You're coming to the Christmas party, aren't you? Oscar's written another play, and some of the other patients are performing."

Promising to attend, I open my bag so the security guard can check it, as he routinely does, for contraband

---

1. People living in the New York City area can do the same thing for free on the first Friday night of any month of the school year. Call Columbia's astronomy department first to confirm.
2. This chapter will appear in a forthcoming issue of *Astrology Guide*. Reprinted by permission of Sterling Publications, Inc.

liquor. He jokes, "Can't you do anything about these stars? They're sure kicking us Taureans around! You'll be using a classroom on the third floor tonight." I promise to try to make those stars behave.

Puffing slightly from the stairs, I arrive to find two of the students, Nick and George, waiting for me. Nick, a big teddy bear of a guy, greets me with a smile. "How's my favorite astrology teacher?" I beam back and ask, "How's life treating you Leos these days?"

"Couldn't be better. Hey, I want you to read this paper I wrote on alcoholism for my sociology class. I did real well on it."

I take the paper to read, but George, too, is demanding my attention. Because of his three planets in Leo and a strong Uranus, George is zany and overdramatic in ways people find hard to take seriously, but I am drawn to the mystic I sense underneath. His chart backs me up, too—several planets in the mystical twelfth house, including a

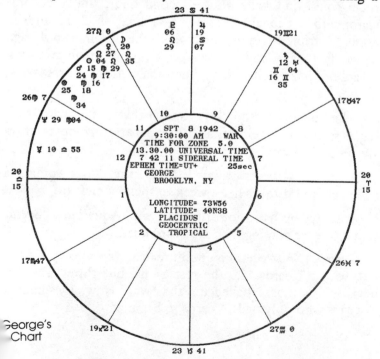

George's
Chart

conjunction of Mars and Neptune. In the past, that conjunction led him to addiction; now he's using it more positively, pursuing spiritual studies with every spare ounce of energy.

George irritates the class with long, involved questions related to himself rather than the topic, so I encourage him to ask before or after class. "I was looking at my chart, and I noticed that all the planets are on the top half. What does that mean?"

"It means you're more involved in big, universal questions than in down-to-earth personal concerns," I answer as the rest of the class troops up the stairs and we get settled in the classroom.

"That sounds like me," George says proudly. I announce, "Class, the observatory will be opening an hour later than we planned. Let's use this time to review."

As usual, there is no chalk or eraser, and I ask if one of them could find some on the second floor. Jim comes forward with a thoughtful present, a box of chalk and an eraser. A triple Scorpio, Jim makes himself felt even though he rarely speaks, and he manages to get as much attention as anyone else, with that silent magnetism Scorpios can have.

The hour passes quickly, as time always does with these eager students. Their humor and penetrating observation always delight me.

"Are all Cancers stingy?" Nick asks. "My woman is a Cancer, and it takes her a week to spend a nickel."

Joe says he has a lot of trouble with Aquarians. "Seems to me they're playing with a 51-card deck."

I agree. "But what you don't realize, Joe, is they started out with 52 cards like the rest of us, but threw one out because it's more challenging that way. Now, I've known Pisceans who only had 51 cards to begin with."

"Hey, teach," George chimes in, "is it true that 75% of Pisceans drink like fish?" For once the class appreciates his wit, and his Leo Moon soaks up the approval.

"The thing about Pisceans is that they're so self-destructive," puts in Sally, who has Pisces rising and knows what she's talking about. "The drinking, I mean. It's like the salmon going upstream to spawn. They know it's going to kill them, but they do it anyway."

"You know, we're joking around about it," says Oscar, the center's playwright, "but astrology is really helping me understand my drinking better. I'm a Capricorn, and they always like to plan far ahead and aim for the top of the mountain, right? Well, that's why I've had so much trouble accepting that A.A. teaching about taking one day at a time. I know their philosophy is good for me, but it sure is hard to practice."

"But I find that astrology helps me with my A.A. work," Nick puts in. "Going through our charts the way we do in class helps me in taking my personal inventory . . . knowing what I have to work on."

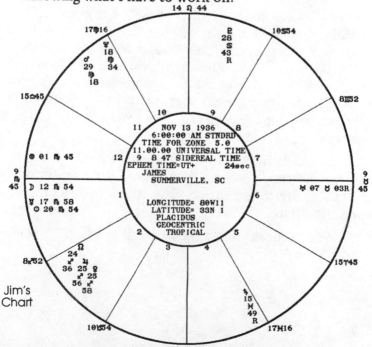

Jim's Chart

"Me too," Jim actually speaks up. "Like when we talked about Mercury and communication, it really hit me how hard it is for me to be open with other people. I have Mercury in Scorpio, and I really have to work at communicating, because if I don't, I feel isolated. I used to have to drink in order to be able to talk to people. Thank God, I'm a little better now."

"What helped me was when we studied the Moon," adds Ron, who has five planets in Moon-ruled Cancer, and the Moon in Scorpio. "I sure never got enough feeding from my mother, and I kept looking for it in all the women I went out with. Naturally, none of them wanted to be a mother to a grown-up man, so they'd get fed up with me and I'd start drinking. Cancers can't handle rejection anyway."

"Yeah, but you can't use being a Cancer as a cop-out," Nick reminds him. "Astrology only shows us what we're like, it doesn't mean we're not responsible for our behavior. Otherwise, it's just another excuse, and you know we learned in health education class that us alcoholics are great at finding excuses for everything."

"You're absolutely right, Nick," I commend him. "Astrology could be a great cop-out if you let yourself use it that way. Like saying, 'I have Neptune on the Ascendant, so I'm fated to drink.' First of all, there are other ways it could work out—you could be a musician or a spiritual teacher. And, second, even if it was working that way at one point in your life, you can always work through from a negative to a positive use of Neptune."

Time speeds by and finally it's time to go. Preparing the class for the trip, I warn, "You know, astronomers don't take too kindly to astrologers. They think we're a bunch of superstitious nuts."

Disbelief echoes around the room. "Say what?" "You're putting us on!"

"I mean it!" I insist.

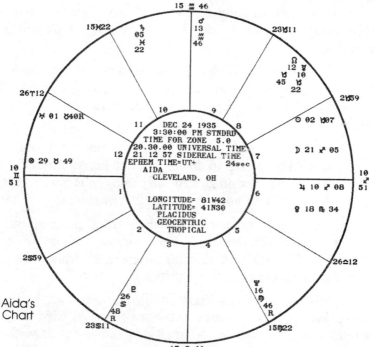

Aida's
Chart

"Look, teach," Aida tries to reason with me. "How can that be? They're working with the planets all the time, and you're trying to tell us they don't believe in astrology? Come on, now! What other reason is there to spend all that time watching the sky?!!" Her prominent Mars in Aquarius shows that Aida can be contentious.

My attempt to explain the mentality of scientists is a dismal failure.

"Then I bet half of them are doing astrology on the sly," Aida concludes. "It just doesn't make sense for them not to believe in it."

I finally fall back on simple authority. "You'll just have to take my word for it, they don't believe in astrology."

When we get ready to leave for Columbia, I discover that many of the students aren't planning to go.

"It's cold out there!" Aida protests. "You know I'm disabled, and I can't make it that far on a night like this."

Aida is always alluding to her disability, but in such a bristly way that I can't ask what she means. It isn't visible, whatever it is.

Nick takes me aside to excuse himself and the others. "Are you going to be mad or hurt if we don't go tonight? I know you Cancers get your feelings hurt easy, but it's really cold."

"No, I really won't be mad. We had a good class tonight anyway, and I'm willing to do whatever the class wants." I'd checked out his paper on alcoholism during lulls in the class, and compliment him now on how well it was written.

George, Jim, and two other men from the class still want to go, so the five of us head for the subway, frosty streamers of breath heralding our progress. We walk briskly, eager for the experience that awaits us.

On the way, Lloyd, a Latin double Scorpio, buttonholes me to ask why people only associate Scorpios with sex. I remind him, "Remember when we talked about how the eighth house and Scorpio were connected with sex? You said sex was a good way to control women. That's very Scorpio, and it's also very chauvinistic."

"Oh, yes, but it's true!" he insists. "The next day they sing and cook and clean up the house. But what else is Scorpio about?"

Shelving the argument, I reply, "It's an intense concern with life and death matters . . . life after death, too. I know you're fascinated with the occult."

At the subway, George puts in a token and bows for me to go through the turnstile. He has Libra rising, and his courtly manners are flattering, but just a fraction too over-done to be taken seriously. On the train, he stands beside me and bends my ear with far-out theories from the latest book he's read. "I read that Jupiter was going to be another star like our sun, but it didn't make it."

"That's Velikovsky's theory," I reply, "and it's interesting, but there's no way to prove it absolutely. Jupiter *is* the biggest planet in our solar system, though. It rules Sagittarius and they love to think big too."

Jim points to Rudolph, who is tall and massively built. "Rudolph is the biggest guy at the center, and he's a Sag."

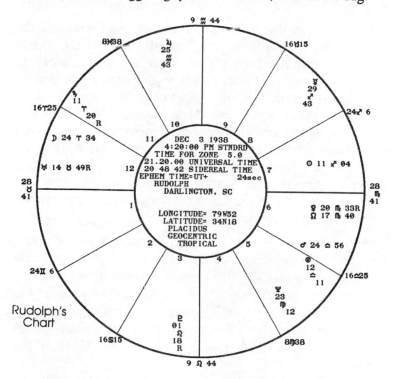

DEC 3 1938
4:20:00 PM STNDRD
TIME FOR ZONE 5.0
21.20.00 UNIVERSAL TIME
20 48 42 SIDEREAL TIME
EPHEM TIME=UT+ 24sec
RUDOLPH
DARLINGTON, SC

LONGITUDE= 79W52
LATITUDE= 34N18
PLACIDUS
GEOCENTRIC
TROPICAL

Rudolph's Chart

Rudolph acknowledges this with good humor and adds, "Today is my birthday, so it's a perfect day for me to look at Jupiter through the telescope."

Lloyd points out that we are getting curious glances from people on the train, and, typically Scorpio, finds a sexual innuendo in it. "They must think you're something special to have so many men with you." Until this moment, I've been so involved in the conversation that it hasn't occurred to me that our group of four black men and one white woman must look a little strange.

"They'd never believe we're going stargazing," puts in quiet Jim. "Tell me, Donna, when is Saturn going to quit doing this number on me?" He's been having heavy Saturn transits to his Scorpio Ascendant, Sun, Moon, and Mercury for months, and for some reason, only the negative side is coming out. I've done about all the positive thinking on it that he or I could swallow, but I try to encourage him again.

We arrive at the gates of Columbia, eagerness and the cold making us hurry. As the five of us climb the stately stone stairway, I suddenly see myself ten years earlier on these same stairs, demonstrating with other discontented Columbia students. My mind pingpongs from that idealistic radical to today's self and back, wondering if I've lost something on the way. I once met an astrotwin of mine, and we'd done different things with our strong Uranus; at the point I went into astrology, on a Uranus transit to Neptune, she joined the Weather people and went off to Cuba. Tonight, looking at the telescope's dome, I decide that astrology was the more rewarding path for me.

Reaching the science building, we take the elevator to the thirteenth floor and climb the remaining flight. From the roof of the building, the view of Manhattan is so beautiful that we forget the sky for a moment. Then we skirt the dome, looking for the door, and somehow manage to lose it. The second trip around in the darkness, we finally get inside and climb a small rickety ladder to the floor of the dome.

"Wow! That telescope's a big mother!" George exclaims.

There were a few other people there—scientific, intellectual types, including a father and his precocious little boy.

"I bet they're wondering why we're here," Lloyd whispers.

"Probably afraid we're going to rip off the telescope," Rudolph grins. We all giggle.

"If they knew it was for astrology, they'd really be uptight," George whispers. We smile conspiratorially and move closer together.

The astronomer operating the telescope first shows us a cluster of three brilliant stars, their full color spectrum visible through the lens.

Jim is amazed. "Now I know why they say 'like a diamond in the sky!' That's just the way diamonds look under a magnifying glass."

"I'm never going to bring my girlfriend here," George says, squinting through the eyepiece. "It'd give her some ideas I couldn't afford."

"What sign do you think this guy that runs the telescope is?" Rudolph whispers to the group.

"Probably Aquarius," Jim whispers back. "They get off on all this science garbage."

"Hey, Mister," George says aloud, "what sign are you?"

Lloyd pokes him, hoping the man hasn't heard. "Hey, man, remember what Donna said."

Full of mischief as ever, George grins and repeats his question, "Hey, Mister, what astrological sign are you?" Lloyd moans.

The astronomer draws himself up indignantly and points up at the sky. "How can you look through my telescope at all this grandness and then talk about superstitious nonsense like that? We're dealing with science here!" Some of the other earnest scientific types who are there titter. "Wooly minded thinkers," one mutters.

"Look, man," Rudolph whispers to George, "Keep quiet before you get us thrown out of here."

"Man's got to be a Virgo," George grins. "Only sign I know of that takes themselves that seriously."

Next the astronomer looks for Jupiter. He pulls a switch and the wooden floor of the dome begins turning, inching noisily into the proper position. When he focuses the telescope this time, a stepladder is needed. "Jupiter has twelve moons," he announces, "but only three of them are visible tonight."

Lloyd fantasizes, "Twelve Moons! Can you imagine looking up in the sky and seeing twelve Moons? You could really sweep a woman off her feet that way!" He climbs up and looks through the eyepiece. "Dios mio! That's beautiful!"

George is next. "Ain't that a blip!" he exclaims.

When I look, I am moved too. Reflected sunlight makes the planet dazzling. A striped pattern is visible on the surface, and the three moons stand out.

Jim looks, then asks, "Why can't we see the rest of the moons?"

"Most of them are on the other side of the planet right now," the man replies, "and some are hard to see tonight because of the atmosphere."

Our own Moon is visible in the slit of the dome right next to Jupiter, so we ask for a look. The astronomer thinks that's boring, but humors us. Craters are visible and the dark part of the Moon is faintly outlined with light.

We hope to see Saturn, and the astronomer calculates the right ascension in his head. "It's risen, but we probably can't see it yet with the lights refracting on the atmosphere." He flicks the switch and the floor moves up, creaking in protest. He swings the telescope's end as high as he can and searches for Saturn. "Ah, here it is."

I get up on the stool, anxious to see it. Saturn is awesomely bright, with those strangely lovely rings surrounding it. "I don't know why," I tell the students, "but I really love that planet." To myself, I add, "It's because you have Venus and Saturn conjunct . . . Venus is love."

George looks next. "Why, it really does have rings! I thought some artist just drew it that way out of his imagination—like a halo around it."

Looking through the scope, Jim says, "This alone is worth the trip. You mean to tell me something that beautiful is causing me all this trouble?"

I ask the astronomer about the recently discovered rings of Uranus. "No, I haven't seen them," he says, "and nothing has come out in any of the astronomy journals about it yet, so they're not official as far as I'm concerned. All I know is what I read in the papers."

The astronomer picks out a few more stars, all as beautiful as the first group, but with different coloring. By this time, our group is freezing, so we descend the rickety stairs to the roof. We pause once more to admire the view of Manhattan and the green ribbon of light that is the George Washington Bridge. I point out the stars and planets we'd seen magnified through the telescope.

"This is really blowing my mind," George says. "A year ago, I was hanging out on the street corner with the guys, drinking wine. If you'd told me then that I'd be at Columbia University tonight, looking through a telescope, I'd have thought you were crazy."

Inside, we warm up a bit before heading back to the subway and Bedford-Stuyvesant. Everyone agrees it has been a beautiful evening.

CRCS PUBLICATIONS

ASTROLOGY, PSYCHOLOGY & THE FOUR ELEMENTS: An Energy Approach to Astrology & Its Use in the Counseling Arts by Stephen Arroyo
.... $7.95 Paperback; $14.95 Hardcover
An international best-seller, this book deals with the relation of astrology to modern psychology and with the use of astrology as a practical method of understanding one's attunement to universal forces. Clearly shows how to approach astrology with a real understanding of the energies involved. Awarded the British Astrological Assn's. Astrology Prize. A classic translated into 8 languages!

ASTROLOGY, KARMA, & TRANSFORMATION: The Inner Dimensions of the Birth-Chart by Stephen Arroyo .... 264 pages, $9.95 Paperback; $17.95 Deluxe Sewn Hardcover
An insightful book on the use of astrology as a tool for spiritual and psychological growth, seen in the light of the theory of karma and the urge toward self-transformation. International best-seller.

RELATIONSHIPS & LIFE CYCLES: Modern Dimensions of Astrology by Stephen Arroyo
.... 228 pages, Paperback $7.95
A collection of articles and workshops on: natal chart indicators of one's capacity and need for relationship; techniques of chart comparison; using transits practically; counseling; and the use of the houses in chart comparison.

REINCARNATION THROUGH THE ZODIAC by Joan Hodgson ..... Paperback $5.50
A study of the signs of the zodiac from a spiritual perspective, based upon the development of different phases of consciousness through reincarnation. First published in England as *Wisdom in the Stars*.

LOOKING AT ASTROLOGY by Liz Greene .... 8½ x 11, $5.95
A beautiful, full-color children's book for ages 6-13. Illustrated by the author, this is the best explanation of astrology for children and was highly recommended by *School Library Journal*. It emphasizes a healthy self-acceptance and a realistic understanding of others. A beautiful gift for children or for your local library.

A SPIRITUAL APPROACH TO ASTROLOGY by Myrna Lofthus ... Paperback $12.50
A complete astrology textbook from a karmic viewpoint, with an especially valuable 130-page section on karmic interpretations of all aspects, including the Ascendant & M.C. A huge 444-page, highly original work.

THE ASTROLOGER'S GUIDE TO COUNSELING: Astrology's Role in the Helping Professions by Bernard Rosenblum, M.D. .... Paperback $7.95
Establishes astrological counseling as a valid, valuable, and legitimate helping profession, which can also be beneficially used in conjunction with other therapeutic and healing arts.

THE JUPITER/SATURN CONFERENCE LECTURES *(Lectures on Modern Astrology Series)* by Stephen Arroyo & Liz Greene .... Paperback $8.95
Transcribed from lectures given under the 1981 Jupiter Saturn Conjunction, talks included deal with myth, chart synthesis, relationships, & Jungian psychology related to astrology.

THE OUTER PLANETS & THEIR CYCLES: The Astrology of the Collective *(Lectures on Modern Astrology Series)* by Liz Greene .... Paperback $7.95
Deals with the individual's attunement to the outer planets as well as with significant historical and generational trends that correlate to these planetary cycles.

CHILD SIGNS: Understanding Your Child Through Astrology by Dodie & Allan Edmands 150 pages, 12 photos of children .... Paperback $6.95
An in-depth treatment of a child's developmental psychology from an astrological viewpoint. Recommended by *Library Journal*, this book helps parents understand and appreciate their children more fully. Nice gift!

DYNAMICS OF ASPECT ANALYSIS: New Perceptions in Astrology by Bil Tierney. Groundbreaking new work! .... 288 pages, Paperback $8.95
The most in-depth treatment of aspects and aspect patterns available, including both major and minor configurations. Also includes retrogrades, unaspected planets & more!

THE PRACTICE & PROFESSION OF ASTROLOGY: Rebuilding Our Lost Connections with the Cosmos by Stephen Arroyo .... late 1984, Paperback $7.95
A challenging, often controversial treatment of astrology's place in modern society and of astrological counseling as both a legitimate profession and a healing process.

A JOURNEY THROUGH THE BIRTH CHART: Using Astrology on Your Life Path by Joanne Wickenburg...168 pages, Paperback $7.95
Gives the reader the tools to put the pieces of the birth chart together for self-understanding and encourages creative interpretation of charts by helping the reader to think through the endless combinations of astrological symbols. Clearly guides the reader like no other book.

THE ASTROLOGY OF SELF-DISCOVERY: An In-Depth Exploration of the Potentials Revealed in Your Birth Chart by Tracy Marks....... 288 pages, Paperback....................................$8.95
A guide for utilizing astrology to aid self-development, resolve inner conflicts, discover and fulfill one's life purpose, and realize one's potential. Emphasizes the Moon and its nodes, Neptune, Pluto, & the outer planet transits. An important & brilliantly original new work!

THE PLANETS & HUMAN BEHAVIOR by Jeff Mayo...180 pp, Paperback $7.95
A pioneering exploration of the symbolism of the planets, blending their modern psychological significance with their ancient mythological meanings. Includes many tips on interpretation!

ASTROLOGY IN MODERN LANGUAGE by Richard B. Vaughan...340 pp, $9.95
An in-depth interpretation of the birth chart focusing on the houses and their ruling planets-- including the Ascendant and its ruler. A unique, strikingly original work! (paperback)

THE ART OF CHART INTERPRETATION: A Step-by-Step Method of Analyzing, Synthesizing & Understanding the Birth Chart...by Tracy Marks. Paperback $7.95
A guide to determining the most important features of a birth chart. A must for students!

For more complete information on our books, a complete booklist, or to order any of the above publications, WRITE TO:

CRCS PUBLICATIONS
Post Office Box 20850
Reno, Nevada 89515-U.S.A.